SELECTED WORKS

OF OLIVIA FREE-WOMAN

olivia free-woman

Acacia Publishing

Selected Works

olivia free-woman

ISBN 978-1-935089-32-2

Library of Congress Control Number: 2010913041

Published by
Acacia Publishing, Inc.
www.acaciapublishing.com

Printed and Bound in the United States of America
First Edition - September 2010

My life is unimportant; what I do with it has infinite significance.

olivia free-woman

Dedication

Fine China and Molotov Cocktails

The women writers' group Fine China and Molotov Cocktails had been meeting twice monthly since June of 1991 (to June 1998). During this time, they have seen each other through creative droughts and eruptions of inspiration, hard re-writes and collaborative compositions. Their writing interests cover a multitude of genres – short fiction, poetry, political analysis, the novel, mysteries, plays and autobiography. They are: Dianne Post, Judy Whitehouse, Paula Waybright and olivia free-woman.

Contents

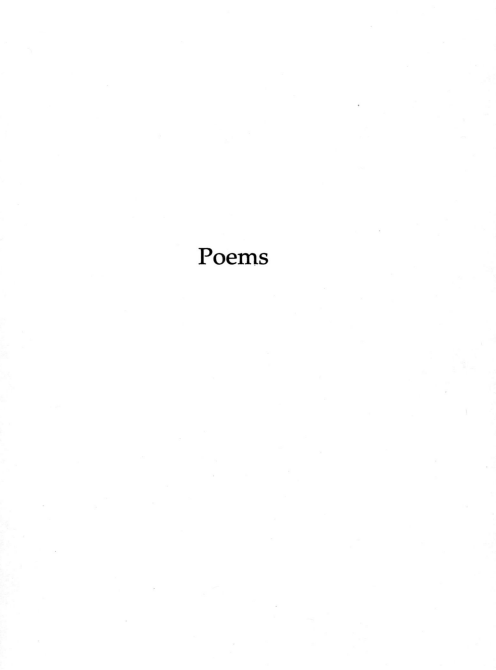

Poems

Living on the Earth

god

It does not matter with whom we align ourselves,
which accidental god of our time we choose;
It is not the position of our deity
that is of importance

Since the advent of our existence,
the disciples of one god have bloodied the Earth
with as much ferocity and regularity as the next.
Congruity, like disparateness, is of little consequence;
Charity has no more hold on one god than another

Whether we dance with serpents or with spirits,
rock to the rhythm of our chants or sit
in silent serenity makes no difference;
The tongue of our prayers holds no bearing

Rather, it is the incidental matters
with which we concern our lives,
the daily encounters, the stance of our existence,
that is the measure of our being

In the interlude between birth and death,
what is believed matters only to the believer;
For all others, the determination of our significance
is in the rendering of our lives.

The Rains

The day before the rains came,
the Earth was covered with crust,
like rust on metal, that crackled
and crumbled underfoot into a fine
feathery powder that billowed
from under the sole

The day before the rains came,
dust covered everything
seeped between crack and crevice
into nostril and under eyelid
until every blink was
like sandpaper against the eye

The day before the rains came,
nothing stirred nor dared to
least the slightest motion
of head or limb shatter the skin
like newsprint left to brittle
under the sun

The day before the rains came,
throats clamped shut and tongues
swollen and fissured clogged mouths
until every breath wheezed with bitter words
past desiccated lips

The day before . . .
dark clouds edged in gold
drops cratered the earth in
soft puffs of dust that tinged the air
with hints of mud

The day before . . .
dark clouds edged in gold dropped
water that cratered the earth in
soft puffs of dust and tinged the air
with hints of mud

The day before . . .
water ran in rivulets drawing
dark figures across stone and branch
cheek and
washing silt from eye and mouth

their skin shattered like newsprint
left out in the sun, shatter with the slightest touch

I think of our loving

I think of our loving
      and the loving of it
Of reaching together
      each other
And the feel of your
      coming in my hands
Of how i melt
      at your finger tips
Wet lips reaching
      crying more
The taste of your being
      lingers on my tongue

Published in a 1983 anthology.

The Wish Blower

rose petals and pansy faces laced
with care in turquoise hands
an offering for a swift journey
wishes written on leaves
and given with dandy lions and

wishes written on leaves and
placed in hands cupped to the
lips of a sun shape face

These are the hands of the wish blower
cupped before laughing eyes

only she knows the way
secret paths traced on winds

with breath of moonlight
and kiss of dawn, she sends
wishes on to the granters of such

with hands cupped before pursed
lips and laughing eyes
of a sun-shaped face

you are the wish blower

only a few know the paths traced
on winds to the granters of wishes

Pomegranates

life broke at her feet
and a thousand tiny
ruby globes
tumbled out

she sampled one
but could not savor its taste
and had no time to make jam
or jelly

she was too busy
ridding the fruit of the hard
kernels that caught in life's
craw and ground like stones
between life's teeth

she had no time to notice
the sweet juice left behind
staining her lips red

Knowledge was her passion
and it dangled before her
enticing but always
out of reach

She chased it anyway
at awkward angles and
down out-of-the-way
passages
marveled by those
who could reach out
and grasp the fruit
just beyond

Never pausing to look
behind
never pausing to see
the swath she had cut
wide and fertile
for others to plant
and others to harvest

The Fence

They took down the fence that kept them apart
Wire strung taunt on wood
pulled and set with muscle and will,
as if metal barbs and wire strands
could keep the dead apart

They took down the fence that kept them apart,
ensured the purity of flesh and stone
from granite and bone,
as though any fence could deter
the worms from wandering

(In the hush of death they came - tiptoeing between
souls who whispered their
collusion in the crush of grass and rattle of tools)

With cutters and snips, shovel and hoe
they dug the ground and
severed the wire 'til
strand after strand gave way,
post after post wobbled free and fell,
and grief rushed past to grief,
sorrow embraced sorrow

They took down the fence that kept them apart
but beyond the reach of
muscle and wire, post and will,
flesh had already mingled with flesh,
bone enfolded on bone,
and serene in the converse of their conspiracy
turned sapling to tree

Splitting Life

in the moment before the phone rang

she was caught,

half way between dishes and laundry,

unsure which to do first and

not wanting to do either,

thinking how nice it would be

if both were just done.

in that moment before the phone rang

she hauled the basket from the bedroom,

shifted towels off the washer

ran water into cereal bowls and emptied

her cup of the last swallow of coffee.

she had no reason to think that that cold coffee

those towels needing folding

the laundry sorted more by use than color

would be the last

the last moment

before the phone rang.

in the moment after the phone rang

a voice she did not know told her

the towels would not be folded

the dishes would be left unwashed

the laundry would not be done.

moments can turn all to rubble

the smell of the boy

the small body damp with sweat

muddied with play

the chipped tooth and scarred chin

the flowers from the neighbor's yard

the neighbor's broken window

the shirt torn in a school yard scuffle

the broken heart from the high school prom

all gone.

the moment before the phone rang

is a memory without memory.

the phone rang and divided life in half.

Writing Clear Thoughts

thought of writing clear thought,
so often what I put down is round in circles;
But it comes to me now that these years
it has not been me who has not written with
distinctness . . . nor has it been my thought that
has been muddied. Rather . . . it is the mode of
presentation available that has not allowed for clarity.

I am trying to describe that odor, that taste — that meets
the mind without words and hangs there trying to be
identified with some memory too far forgotten and can
only be said to be . . . familiar.

Familiar — a knowing — that which is in common
with self . . . with . . .
    (There are no words beyond the dots)
                    . . . with that which is.

And I am here again in that space so vacant yet so full
And I feel and cannot say; I speak with other women
and though I can not say it they too know
and we speak of it by unclear means.

Energy.
        And connectedness.
                    Goddess.

And it passes as identified until we go too far
for the words to follow and we stumble.

We feel it and we know it and we almost see it. And we **stop.**

There is somewhere an opening. There is no going
through it. Only a growing into it.

And we are not yet green enough.
Another fall to come. Another winter of hidden growth.
And the forest continues if only by the seeds it sows.

I could have changed the world

I could have changed the world
in the time I've wasted
Charted a course others would follow
Dreamt a dream others would live

I could have leveled the dams
replanted the trees
turned back the highways
to the prairie dogs and the weeds
made the everyday pressings of war
the memories of a generation ago

I could have changed the world
in the time I've wasted
Done something worth
the price of an hour

Many people have said that indeed, she did change the world
both with her teaching and her activism. And perhaps with
her words.

If I take but one

if I take but one
one time, one moment,
one instance

if I take but one
one thought, one notion,
one tenet

if I take but one
one memory, one sorrow,
one love

to whom would I bequeath the rest?

i am all and inseparable
no leftovers, no
spare parts

if I take but one
then I take all

Feminism, Racism and War

Fire brand burns – A choral poem

Fire brand burns
like an eye in the night
Like the moon that has waxed
or Polaris at her height

To the mother it is warmth
To the witch it is strength
But in the hand of the man
only death does it bring

In the flash of an atom
in the flare of a match
He has moved towards destruction
from the flint he first scratched

It breathes down our necks
and laps at our skirts
Eats at our flesh
and devours our works

"Put the torch to the child,
let the witches be damned.
Melt down the goddess
for the power of man!"

But the breath of a woman
on a low burning coal
White hot in the darkness
fans the flames of the soul

And our voices are carried
on smoldering winds
"Let then burn! Let them burn!
These institutions of men!

"No more brides without dowries,
no more widows on pyres.
No mother nor child
as fuel for their fires!"

And the breath of a woman
on a low burning coal
White hot in the darkness
fans the flames of the soul

(repeat)

The <u>ash</u> of a woman's dream
                I am a woman
The <u>ash</u> of a woman's child
                I am alive
The <u>ash</u> of a woman's hands
                I am a woman
The <u>ash</u> of a woman's life
                I will survive

(This poem is read in three-parts. One reading the verse, on the second reading, a voice joins repeating the chorus "And the breath of a woman ..." throughout, and on the third reading, the third voice joins reading the four "ash" parts.)

He feels like a woman who has been raped.

He feels like a woman who has been raped
He says he feels like a woman
who has been raped
So fine in the prime of his life
when misfortune befalls him
And he feels like a woman who has been raped

So tell me, man,
What does it feel like to feel like a woman
who has been raped?

Do you feel abused, misused
mistreated and defeated?
Like you got a bum's rush
and were all trussed up and beaten?

Do you feel misled, bled dry
left nowhere to die
alone every bone in your body broken?

What does it feel like to feel like a woman
who has been raped?

Do you feel filthy, dirty, hurting
so deep inside you can't hide
even from the strangest stranger?

Do you feel negated, hated
pissed on and pissed off
with no where to shove your anger
but back down deep inside you?

Do you feel hit upon, tread upon
invaded, degraded unable to face
a coming day without dread or
just plain dead. What does it feel like to feel
like a woman who has been raped?

He says he feels like a woman
who has been raped
And I, what would I have to do
to know what it feels like
to feel like a man who feels like a woman
who has been raped

Hey, man
Don't come to me for your sympathy
I have none for you
Because I know...
I know what it feels like to feel like a woman
who has been raped

I know women - I

I know a woman whose husband
                    forbids her to eat
He rations the money
     just enough for food
          just enough for himself and their daughter

He takes her to work
          each day she minds the store
                    while he leaves for lunch

Her daughter sneaks in hamburgers
     if it is a weekend or she doesn't have to be at school

She died
in the morning light rising
          making coffee cooking for him
                    frying eggs bacon toast

She died
showering dressing slipping
          blouse slip skirt
                    over sharp-edged bones ankles wrists

She died
cleaning up quickly clearing dishes
               hurrying behind him
                    kissing her daughter good bye

She died

11 Aug. 1987

I know women – II

I know women
     who are dying
         and I don't know what to do

I have fantasies
  Of pink helmets in Japan and Karate stances in Peru
Of bands of women in the upper plains states
occupying homes
     until *he* decides it would be easier simply to leave
Of neatly bandaged men found on hospital door steps,
                    disarmed

 I have called the police to say,
        I know he has a gun
    It is in his car.

And have heard them say,
         That is not illegal.

I have called the police to say,
     I know he is going to kill her
      I heard him say so.

And have heard them say,
         But she will not leave.

I have called the police to say,
     I know he is a rapist
      I have heard him brag.

And have heard them say,
         But we have no victim.

Sometimes,
    we know,
        the only way to save a woman's life is...

Sometimes,
    we know,
        the only way
            to save a woman's life is...

Sometimes,
    we know
        the only way
            to save a woman's life
                    is...

Sometimes
    we know
        the only way
            to save a woman's life.

1987

Birmingham, Alabama, September, 1963

There was no equal chance
      no random selection
No accidental opportunity

This wasn't a lottery with
      black spots on folded paper
Narrowing first to family
      then victim

There was no drawing of lots

On that morning
      that Sunday morning
Before music played and
      voices raised above open hymnals
Before pews filled and
      aisles rustled with crinoline
and starched shirts

There were only those
      who would be there

That their names were unknown
      their faces invisible
does not make their deaths

Random

Not by chance
       but by appointment
Not by accident but
       with purpose
Not by force of some
       unpredictable circumstance
But with force
And for the clearly reasoned
       circumstance of their lives

He still corresponds

"He still corresponds with a few of his former inmate students, including one who murdered several women in a beauty shop, and who Johnson feels is one of the most gifted student writers he has ever met."*

There is no gift, no gifted

HE TOLD THEM TO LIE FACE DOWN IN A CIRCLE
THEIR HEADS TOWARD HIM

just the day to day putting down and
putting up with

HE STOOD AT CENTER...
MOVED LIKE CLOCK WORK

There is no gift

> FIRING,
> TURNING
> FIRING,
> TURNING

just the knowing that today does not
necessarily mean tomorrow will come

> FIRING,
> TURNING

There is no gift

FROM ONE TO ANOTHER LIKE THE HANDS OF A CLOCK HE MOVED

just the birth, the dying and the dying

FIRING OFF THEIR LIVES

again

The title of this poem is from an article on award-winning local poet Denis Johnson that appeared in the Arizona Republic on May 9, 1982.
Previously published in an anthology in 1983.

Tangled spiral

We are mindful of our differences . . .
        . . . and distances:
Outstretched arms
cannot touch the feel of you;
Slender fingers, unwebbed, cannot
cup your breath to my lips.

It is a tangled spiral of thread
that has drawn us upward;
From swamp mud we've climbed,
sucked in cold breaths, gasped
as we humped higher 'til erect,
we stretched forth slender fingers . . .
        separate
                and unwebbed . . .
Eyes set straight ahead,
there is no guessing at what is in front of us;
We are mind-full and soul searching,
yet cannot see who is beside us.

We see only straight ahead.

We are predetermined . . .
        the height of our stature,
                the breadth of our nose,
                        the thickness of our hair . . .
Each garners greater credence
than all the wisdom, creativity
and compassion we can muster;
Our minds, curious though they may be,
are easily bloodied;

Saturated to the point of apathy,
we stack our disdain six feet deep and turn
our backs in indifference;
We cannot face what is behind us . . .
      we stare only straight ahead;

We have not the intellect
to know our ignorance is not innocence;
To see you, I must turn . . .
      my mind,
          my eyes,
              my direction . . .
To know you, I must transform.

When the froth is gone,
when the steam has vanished,
do all wars boil down to
a single thread from that tangled spiral?
What is it the cells discern?
      The breadth of your nose;
          The thickness of your hair;
              The height of your stature?
Can the cells truly tell the Croat from the Serb;
The Hutu from the Tutsi?

. . . or . . .

Can they feel what I
cannot touch, see what I
cannot find in front of me;
Is there within them some
fragment of thread encrusted still
with swamp mud, yet able to drag forth,
            reach out,
                        hands cupped,
to draw your breath to my lips?

Perhaps . . .

Within this clatter about us,
this clanging of threads, these stacks
that amass six feet deep behind our backs,
there is a croaking from the mud:
            A hope . . .
                        yet wingless . . .
                                    clawing to come forth.

MARY ESTHER

This knotted child is really a woman
of sixteen   and i know her poverty
has as much to do with this so-called
medical miracle as the meningitis

that drew   her thighs to her chest   her
breast bone away from her spine   her
fingers   hands   arms   in upon herself

she can not see   she does not hear

i think maybe she can smell   her
gaping grimace opens stretching
white strands of saliva between
cracked lips as odors are passed
beneath her nostrils

i know she cries   when food
slipped through a tube into her
stomach gurgitates   up her
throat   out her mouth   her
nose   or perhaps it's just
tears   eyes watering
the way they do for onions
or methyelate

i turn her body from one side
to the other side and back   again
in an effort to prevent sores
i do not know she would feel

i change her diaper   clean
excrement from her buttocks   menses
from her pubic hair   urine
from crevices between her legs

i tilt her head back   dribble water
down her throat as she gags   tongue
thrusting forward   i listen
to wheezed sounds   graveled moans
air breathed out

This knotted child is really a woman
of sixteen   i cradle in my arms   hold
to my breast   stroke   caress   rock

and i wonder   if these tears i
see now   this grimace that opens
stretching   this moan that breaths
out   is for the smell
of my arms   around
this knotted woman

4 July 1986

Farm Labor

Did you ever stop to ask,
From where did these grapes come?
Did you ever stop to think,
Whose hand held this peach?
Whose back ached under the weight
of these apples?
How did this food get to your table,
into your hand, into your mouth?
Whose toil was it?
Whose sweat fell, whose muscles throbbed,
whose child waited alone,
at home, so that you could
savor this grape, this peach,
this apple.
This salad, this lettuce,
these carrots
the broccoli, the peppers, this onion
this melon, these pecans,
this pear.
Each held by the hand,
passed through the fingers
of a mother, a son,
someone's father,
their daughter.
Whose soul was tinted
with soil,
whose hopes were soiled with
the labor, that feeds you now.

This is for Eric

This is for Eric
and I know you don't want to hear that
because Eric was just some
gang-banging two-bit punk
who made the mistake
of giving a cop some alias of a name
that just happened to be the name
of some other two-bit punk
with an arrest warrant

and instead of getting arrested –
he shot him, Eric did –
shot the cop and killed him
and then highjacked some guy
in a car and made it to the west side
before the cops caught up with him
holding the guy hostage –
he shot him, Eric did –

and shot him, the cops did –
shot Eric and killed him

Yeah – like I said
you didn't want to hear
that this is for Eric

But before Eric was a punk
before he was a gun toting
two bit gang banger with violence
streaking down his back
he was somebody's kid

like so many other kids
who come toddling and running
walking and carried across the border
by parents who want
nothing more for them than
something beyond a sixth grade education
a chance not to have to work quite so hard
the possibility of owning their own home
the opportunity to have things a little better

so this is for Eric
even if his parents didn't get
what they wanted

But,
this is also for Dara
came here in her mother's arms
struggled in school, made it to graduation
working now
caretaker of her older sister
advocate for homeless teens
she will give a presentation to your group
if you're interested

And this is for Mariana
who hasn't seen Venezuela
since she was six
and who can't see college because
twelve years here doesn't make you a resident
and out of state tuition is just too high
for even community college when
any moment you might not have a job

And this is for German
so excited to be done with high school
ready and eager to join the military
wanting to serve his country
only his country doesn't want him
so he has no country to serve

And this is for Eli
who can't wait for any Dream Act
because she's almost thirty now
and even if it does pass she'll be too old
and if she's sent back she'll leave behind
a mother and sister because
when her mother married
she was too old then too
so didn't get papers and
couldn't get citizenship

And this is for Jesus
who at sixteen was living
on his own, working full time
taking honor classes in high school
until La Migra pulled him over
took his truck, dropped him
across the border without
even the money from his pocket

Yeah
this is for Eric
and Dara
and Mariana
and German
and Eli
and Jesus

Because all of them are somebody's kids
Because all of them should be ours

December 2007

To the man who did not like the sign on my car so

yelled "alien"

Sixteen-ninety
Sixteen hundred and ninety
That's when Cornelius Kincheloe
wed a Miss Williams
somewhere in Virginia

aliens in a foreign land
by what law were they legal
by what right was this law imposed
by outsiders on a land they did not own

Nancy Jo Kincheloe
the great, great, great I don't know
how many greats granddaughter
of Cornelius

one of Austin's three-hundred
aliens settling a foreign land
legal by law imposed by a government
on a land they did not own

Nancy Jo Kincheloe
mother to Luis Lamar Green
my great grandfather

took his family and bribed
their way into Mexico
aliens in a foreign land
most certainly illegal

what papers allowed them back in
what papers declared their right to enter
not as aliens, not as immigrants, but with
inherent rights

yes, I am an alien and
we are all aliens
intruders on land taken at one time
by laws imposed by those who
were without the right to impose
such laws

and we welcome you – an alien

9-11

there is no name yet

    Intifada

    Holocaust

    Watts Riots

    Haymarket Uprising

    Whiskey Rebellion

only long phrases that walk around it

    Since New York

    After September

    Prior to the Eleventh

    Before the World Trade Center

the name will come later

it will slip into the vernacular

quietly, gently,

without the devastation of its consequence

unnoticed and all-embracing

Ruby Slippers

There are ruby slippers amongst the shoes at Auschwitz
Red leather gems amid the black, brown and gray

Scarlet cloth summer shoes for toes to peak through
Shiny patent leather now tainted with dust

There are ruby slippers amongst the shoes at Auschwitz
Silent shoes waiting no heels clicking

Silent shoes waiting

There's no place like home

It is too much

Sometimes it is just too much . . .
To know the who, the what, the where
(There is no why)

Yet, I look again
to see the faces rigid in fear,
the bodies, stripped naked of dignity
the eyes staring, piercing the lens

It is too much to know

But, I look again
to see the children

And, I look yet again
to see the bodies sculpted by flame
the bodies slung in piles like waste
the bodies strewn about like litter

To know . . . the who, the what, the when.

*In 2008, olivia was chosen by the National Endowment of the
Arts for a Holocaust Tour to travel to Washington, D.C. and
several countries in Europe where she visited concentration
camps and memorials to learn better how to incorporate
teaching of the Holocaust in middle school. These poems were
written after that visit.*

For Children

My Favorite Color Is Balloon

My favorite color? What is it you ask?
That assuredly is a most difficult task.
Which color's my favorite when all's done and said?
I guess I would say it is definitely . . .

Red!

Red is an apple ready to eat;
The color of sky when sea and sun meet;
Roses are red and cherries are, too.
My favorite color most certainly is . . .

Blue!

When I look up I see a blue sky.
Blue birds and blue jays sing as they fly.
There are lakes with blue water and blue waves that go
smack!
My favorite color has got to be . . .

Black!

Black is the night when stars shine and twinkle;
The color of clouds when rain starts to sprinkle;
The small bat that squeaks, the great bear that bellows!
No question about it, my favorite is . . .

Yellow!

Bananas and pears are both yellow in color.
And yellow is even the color of butter.
Yellow leaves in the fall, yellow camp fires at night;
My favorite color has got to be . . .

White!

Big puffy clouds that float overhead;
Cold winter snow to slide down on sleds;
Lightening that flashes with big booming sounds;
There isn't a doubt, my favorite is . . .

Brown!

Brown is the mud I love to play in;
The color of branches I love to hide in;
Brown deer and dogs and rabbits I've seen;
When it comes right down to it, my favorite is . . .

Green!

There are little green worms that eat green leaves
That grow on the branches of big green trees.
And green is the color for grass that is used.
My favorite color? I'm so confused!

Is it red like an apple or white like the snow?
Is it blue? Is it black? Is it brown? I don't know!
Bananas are yellow, but grass is so green,
And the sky's every color that I've ever seen!

There's elephant grey and orange as in oranges.
I make up my mind then my mind up and changes.
Lavenders, pinks, turquoise, chartreuses;
There are so many colors with so many uses!

I wish I could decide which color I like,
But I can't, though I try and I try all my might.
If there was just one color instead of so many
I would choose that color as better than any.

One color so pale it would be the color of light;
One color so dark it would be the color of night;
A color with everything from mauve to maroon!
My favorite color will just have to be . . .

BALLOON!

My Best Friend

Who would you like as your best friend,
To share all your secrets, to play and pretend?
Someone better than the other friends you've got . . .
What do you think?

I'd rather not.

How about a friend who flies to the stars,
One that can take you to Saturn or Mars;
A friend who flies spaceships, your own astronaut!
Is this who you want?

I'd rather not.

How about a writer for your best friend;
One who tells stories and loves to pretend;
A friend with the most creative thoughts . . .
How about a writer?

I'd rather not.

Your very best friend could be a clown,
With big happy smiles and painted on frowns;
A clown who does tricks with mops, brooms and pots.
Would you want a clown?

I'd rather not.

An explorer could show you different new places,
Mountains and canyons and wideopen spaces;
Glaciers that are frozen and deserts that are hot.
Would you want an explorer?

I'd rather not.

How about an actor who stars on T.V.,
One other people go to movies to see;
The star of every show, the hero of every plot!
Is this who you want?

I'd rather not.

A scientist knows so many things
About rainbows and airplanes and how bees sting.
A scientist for a friend could teach you a lot.
Is this who you want?

I'd rather not.

What an interesting friend a ship's captain would be,
You could sail o'er the waves of oceans and seas
On huge ocean liners or brave, tiny yachts.
How about a captain?

I'd rather not.

I've gone through the list from bottom to top,
Every friend I've suggested, you'd rather not.
Just who do you think your best friend should be?

My very best friend ought to be . . . **ME!**

1999

Schnebly Cruthers

Schnebly Cruthers refused breakfast
Not milk, toast, cereal or eggs.

While his sister ate pancakes,
Schnebly just dangled his legs.

"Schnebly," said his mother, "You must eat a bite."
But Schnebly ate nothing, his teeth he clenched tight.

Then Schnebly and his sister hurried off to school
His stomach still empty, her stomach so full.

It was later that morning, just 'bout 'round ten
When in the middle of math, there came a mighty rumblin'

"Schnebly!" said the teacher. "Was that noise from you?
You didn't eat breakfast this morning, did you?"

Schnebly said nothing, but his stomach, it grumbled.
It growled and it gurgled, it tumbled and rumbled.

"Schnebly," said the teacher. "Keep your stomach quiet.
Your not eating breakfast is no cause for a riot!"

Given a direction, Schnebly always obeyed it,
So he folded his math and quietly ate it.

But his stomach still rumbled, grumbled and churned,
So he decided to feed it something else he had learned.

He pulled out his science and tasted a bit,
But his science couldn't begin to fill up the pit.

He opened his book, ate chapters two, three and four,
But his stomach still gurgled. It still wanted more!

He reached for a workbook, nibbled a chart,
Rolled up a map, found a Valentine heart.

He ate his books bite by bite
Until his teacher yelled in a fright.

"Schnebly Cruthers, what did you do?
Go to the office. You can't eat the school!"

The principal looked at Schnebly and frowned.
"You didn't eat breakfast, so its paper you down?"

"You can not eat textbooks, Schnebly Cruthers.
You leave me no choice. I'm calling your mother."

"Sit here in this chair and don't you dare move,
While I tell your mother how you're eating the school."

But just as the principal picked up the phone
The secretary barged in and said with a moan,

"Ms. Marble, come quick! Come look at this mess!
Schnebly Cruthers has eaten my desk!"

Where files and messages once could be seen
Was the top of a desk, perfectly clean.

"Find Schnebly! Quickly! And quietly, too!
We don't want to alarm the rest of the school."

"Go get his sister. And call up his mother.
Perhaps they can help us with Schnebly Cruthers."

"Mrs. Cruthers, I say this full of dread,
But your young son, Schnebly eats paper," she said.

"And the copy machine's empty. All the paper is gone.
We've got to stop Schnebly if school's to go on!"

But soon the word spread throughout the schoolyard
That Schnebly Cruthers had eaten the report cards!

"Go Schnebly!" a young girl declared.
The students all clapped, the teachers all glared.

"Someone stop Schnebly! Don't be such cowards.
We won't have a school if the paper's devoured!

"Check every classroom, every cranny and nook.
And warn the librarian he may be after her books!"

Schnebly stood hiding by room forty-four
Just down the hall from the library door.

His stomach still rumbled, grumbled and growled,
And he thought of the books that the library housed.

The librarian, forewarned, gave a menacing look,
As she stood by the door guarding her books.

But with his rumbling stomach encouraging him,
He slipped through her legs and Schnebly was in!

He ran for the fiction. He started with Z.
He ate through the X's, the S, R's and T's.

He went for the O's, the NML's and K's
He ate through the F's the EDC's, B's and A's.

"Stop!" the librarian cried. But Schnebly wouldn't listen.
He turned his attention to the Dewey Decimal System.

Through geology, biology and botany he ravaged.
Biography, geography, psychology, he was savage.

Soon the library shelves were eaten clean through,
Fiction, non-fiction, and references too.

On the shelves where Schnebly had been so rampageous
Forlorn book covers stood totally pageless.

The teachers, the students, his sister and mother
all stood and stared at Schnebly Cruthers

The principal and teachers consoled the librarian,
When his sister declared, "Listen! It's quiet again!"

No rumble, no grumble, no gurgle, no growl,
Schnebly Cruthers was not hungry now.

School wasn't canceled. It always goes on
Even if homework must be written till dawn.

The books in the library were eventually replaced.
Though Schnebly still isn't allowed in the place.

Schnebly Cruthers, what did he learn from all this?
Does he still skip his breakfast or eat like his sis?

He still has a problem, infected with a pox,
His sister eats cereal, and Schnebly eats the box.

Short Stories

Meatloaf

Life was not his forte. It had always seemed that even the little tasks life required and everyone else mastered so easily demanded from him a bravery he would never quite muster. As a result, he negotiated each day as if it were a swirling river with rapids and sinkholes intent on swallowing him whole.

That's how he saw himself now, standing outside the diner, studying the currents inside, deciding how best to navigate them to the counter along the opposite wall.

The cowbell overhead clanked as the door brushed past it. He hesitated, wiped the sweat from his palms, then dove into the clatter of blue-plate specials and truck driver guffaws that rattled the room in the glare of fluorescent lights. A waitress in pink with a white ruffled apron whirled past him, and a man with grease-stained hands suddenly loomed in front, but he sidestepped them both and landed safely on the other side.

The stool, as always, was too tall for his stature, but from tiptoe he could ease himself onto it without too much notice. He gripped the counter and settled in, his squat body clinging to the edges of the stool like wax gone cold on a candle.

"Coffee?"

He looked up. The pink and white waitress had "Alice" pinned to her shoulder. The coffee pot hung in midair over a cup balanced in her other hand.

"Yes, please." Before the whisper was out he wished he could have it back.

"Was that a yes?" Her voice scraped above the clamor around him.

He cleared his throat and pushed his reply out. "Yes."

The cup dropped in front of him, and the coffee rushed up its sides before settling into its middle.

"Here you go, Al." The figure behind him leaned over his shoulder and plopped a five and change onto the countertop.

Alice wadded the money into her free hand. "You take it easy, Rick, ya hear? An' don't you give that wife of yours anymore grief or it'll be me you'll be answering to."

"Better listen to her, Rick." The words pushed in from the other side. "Al's the last person you ever want to answer to."

The room thundered with laughter. Beneath it all, he tried to remember why he had come.

"Meatloaf."

He looked up. Hunks of men reflected from the stainless steel behind the counter, rattling at tables and chairs. Boulder-like, they rumbled together, bouncing back slaps and raucous laughter off one another. His figure stood out, distinct in its roundness, a balding head plopped between soft plump shoulders.

How did he get himself into this mess? It was a stupid question. The answer was reflected in front of him. He studied the counter again.

"Meatloaf."

"Not today. Meatloaf's Monday. Today is Wednesday. Wednesday's tuna melt."

He looked up. Alice stood in front of him, her pencil poised over her pad. A pink bubble emerged from between her lips and popped loudly. "Ya want the tuna melt?"

The empty stool beside him spun and came back around full of jeans and t-shirt. "Hey, Alice. Ya meet my friend? This here's Carl. We used to work together, but now we're partners. Yes, sir. An' we're gettin' rich together. Ain't that right, Carl?" The arm around Carl's shoulders pulled him hard to the side, and he grabbed the counter to keep from being pulled off the stool.

Carl focused on his hands, his knuckles white as they gripped the Formica in front of him. His mouth went dry and he struggled to form the words. "You told me Meatloaf."

"Not today. Meatloaf's Monday. Today is Wednesday. Wednesday's tuna melt." The same pink bubble pushed its way out from between Alice's lips and exploded.

"Meatloaf?" Carl waited for the word to sink in. "Meatloaf! You idiot!" The jeans and tee-shirt jumped to his feet. "It was Meatball! I told you Meatball!"

"Not today. Meatball's Friday. Today is Wednesday. Wednesday's tuna melt."

Carl looked past Alice to the boulders in the stainless steel. They had stopped their rumbling. He could hear a single spoon clunk inside a coffee cup at the end of the counter; the hum of a fan in the kitchen layered in the background between the tapping of a boot behind him.

"You put it all on Meatloaf?" The jeans and tee-shirt leaned into Carl, grabbing the collar of his jacket.

Carl nodded. The fists pulled him closer. "I oughta . . ."

63

Carl waited. Alice, pencil still in hand, blew another bubble. Out of the corner of his eye, he could see the boulders, still, silent, waiting.

"You S.O.B.!" The jeans and tee-shirt shoved him back. Carl hugged the counter to keep from loosing his balance. When he looked back, the jeans and tee-shirt were gone.

Clatter rose from behind him. He looked in the stainless steel and the boulders were moving, jostling each other again. Carl looked at Alice. The bubble popped and she sucked the gum back in between her lips. He slipped his hand into the pocket of his jacket, wrapped his fist around the wad of bills secreted there and squeezed.

"I'll have the tuna melt, please."

Rae Jean

Rae Jean squatted in the alley behind her house, the back of her plaid skirt brushing the muddy ruts behind her. She would hear about it later, about how dirty she was, why it was a waste of money to pay the nuns to teach her when she couldn't even learn to keep herself clean.

Just now, though, it was the small black form lying in the weeds that held her attention. One leg splayed out awkwardly in the wrong direction and specks of dirt clung to the wide unseeing eyes. She ran her hand over the cat's head and down its back, its flesh stiff beneath her fingertips. No more purrs, she thought, but deep in her own throat, somewhere down inside what she called the "pit of me" there was a rumble.

She took the white handkerchief the nuns said proper ladies kept tucked up the sleeve of their sweaters and spread it over the cat's body. She wouldn't cry. She knew that. But with each breath, she felt the rattle growing deep inside.

Rae Jean pushed the gate open over the weeds that grew knee high on either side of it and waded through to the back porch. She picked up the battered plastic bowl that sat on the top step and dumped the remains of its contents onto the ground.

In the kitchen, her father sat at the metal table, its Formica top long ago chipped away. Rae Jean didn't look at him, but watched from inside as his eyes followed her across the room. She set the bowl in the sink and ran a slow dribble of water into it, then reached through the curtain that hung from the edge of the counter and pulled an almost empty box of cat food out from behind it.

Her father's chair creaked as he leaned forward into the table and toward her. She tossed the box into the trashcan.

She turned to look at him. His temples pulsed as he ground his teeth together, but it was his eyes she wanted. Those dark eyes that stood out against the yellow skin around them. Those dark eyes that glazed over whenever he humped his body against hers in the dun of night.

She found them. Found them and held them to hers in a knot so tight she was almost sure it would strangle him. But he grunted, half laughed, and the knot was severed. She turned her back toward him and headed for the door that led down the hall.

"You filthy bitch." She stopped. "Look at you. Shit hangin' off you like some fuckin' dog. I don't know why I waste the money."

Rae Jean waited, but he had nothing else to say. Inside, deep down in the pit of her, she could feel the thunder, still low, but ever growing.

....

The door pushed through a thick veil of smoke and into the low din of male voices.

"Ya want smoking or non?" The woman at the booth

didn't look up from the cards whose rough edges she shuffled together and then laid out in front of her.

"Non."

The woman pointed to the other side of the room without bothering to look up. A lattice of brown wood laced with plastic grape leaves feigned a wall impenetrable to the smoke.

Rae Jean crossed to the other side and sat at a booth. The high pitch of a country singer battled from the juke against the spin of the wheel on the television over the lunch counter. A waitress appeared at the table.

"I'll have coffee an' two eggs, scrambled . . . with hash browns." Before she could look up, the waitress had already filled her cup and was gone.

Despite their tight jeans and ten-gallon hats, the men at the counter didn't look like cowboys to Rae Jean. They were too hard. Their words clanked together like metal, didn't chafe like leather on leather. Grease was the only stain their boots knew.

The plate slid in front of her, butter glassy across the top of the eggs. The coffee she had managed to sip was replaced, and the woman was gone again.

A no-tipper. Her mom used to complain about old men and kids who never left much of a tip, if any at all. People got kids. Don't they know that? No waitress job pays shit but for the tips.

She only had six dollars left, but she knew she would leave a tip, if only because she never wanted to face her mother this side or the other and have to say she didn't.

Three dollars and forty-eight cents. And if she left ten percent that'd be three eighty-five. She'd barely have two dollars left. She thought about leaving a note, but heard her mother's voice again. A note don't feed the devil.

A no-tipper. She left three bills and two quarters under the saucer's edge and made her way through the smoke to the door.

....

The man on the other half of the car seat stared at his fingers playing in front of him. Rae Jean kept her eyes low, glancing only occasionally at the short, chubby fingers that prattled back and forth between themselves.

She made herself chew, forcing the dry hamburger past the lump in her throat until she was afraid she wouldn't be able to keep any more down. She crumpled the paper around what was left and shoved it back into the sack.

"I'll save the rest 'til later."

"You're sure?" The man's voice was low with a squeak that made it sound like he had to work to keep it baritone. "I can wait."

But Rae Jean couldn't. She shook her head. She set the sack on the floorboard next to her feet and started to unbutton her blouse.

"I'll do that."

Rae Jean laid her hands at her sides and closed her eyes. The man's fingers stumbled over the buttons as he leaned across her, his breath a coarse whistle in her ear.

As he parted her blouse, she opened her eyes and stared out the window. The night was clear, and the stars lay in a deep, white mantle overhead. The Milky Way.

His hands scraped against her thighs as he lifted her skirt.

A billion stars to count.

He rammed against her, his over-sized body wedging

between her legs. The stars thickened, and the window crank dug into her back.

His zipper scoured her leg, and he shared his satisfaction in short heavy grunts. The stars faded to a blanket of white.

Rae Jean squeezed her arm from between him and the back of the seat. She reached toward the heavens and touched the cold, wet glass. She pointed her finger and trailed it through the Milky Way. R-A-J-E. Raje. And the stars sparkled through.

1993

A Tear in the Sky

If there had been clouds, rain clouds, storm clouds, even white fluffy ones, she might have thought it was lightning. But there weren't any. Just a haze smeared across the sky and pulled thin enough in places for the blue to show through.

She glanced back to where she had seen it. To her left, it had started, high over her shoulder, then ripping down toward the crest of the mountain and beyond . . . a tear in the sky.

It had been there only an instant, a white blazing crevice tearing downwards then sealing itself back up, over-lapping its edges, she was sure, for how else could a tear so frayed be healed? She stared, squinting, trying to see the seam, the ripple in the fabric that must now be there, but she saw nothing.

Then another thought crossed her mind. What had caused it? Pollution? A hole in the ozone layer? Rotted fabric giving way like sheets hung too often in the sun to dry? Or perhaps some thing pressed against the boundaries, clawing its way through, trying to get out, or get in.

The horn behind her brought her back to the green light and the cars pulling away in front of her. She shifted into gear and pulled slowly forward.

Who else had seen it, she wondered. She looked around,

but no one else's attention seemed drawn to the mountain's peak. Perhaps it would be on the news tonight, some reassuring, logical explanation to soothe the panic that such an event must bring.

She glanced once more at the space above the mountain and now saw it. A line, crooked and jagged, only slightly bluer than the sky around it, traversing the path the tear had taken.

She planned her evening around the news that night. Fed the cat, washed her hair, and then curled up in front of the television with a bowl of cold cereal. Cooking was not her strong point.

The lead story was about a child who had slipped through a sewer grate and had been pulled to safety by two men who just happened to have been arguing over a fender bender nearby. It was followed by an update on the upcoming city council election. Then there was a four vehicle accident that amazingly had no fatalities, a walk-a-thon to raise money for some disease and . . .

"Citizens flooded the capital today with calls concerning a possible invasion." The man on television was straightening his papers. "We'll have that and other stories after these messages."

She poured herself another bowl of cereal, let the cat in and sat back down in front of the television. The cat rubbed against her leg in anticipation of a bowl to lick clean.

But the news story concerned only an invasion of insects and the damage they might pose for people's gardens.

She flipped through the other channels, but it was too late. She caught only the scores of games played and the latest news on players injured and traded.

She turned the television off, gave the cat her bowl and went to bed. But it was a long time before she slept and then it was a fretful sleep filled with dreams of things fraying. She ran panicked in them, gathering needle and thread, thread and needle, trying to sew back together the clothes that fell from her, the walls that ripped from the foundations, the trees and stones that tore from the earth, until it was her own skin that frayed and fell away from her body as she tried desperately to slip the thread through the eye of the needle and sew it back on to her. She awoke earlier than usual, exhausted but grateful.

It would not do any good for her to search the skies as she drove to work. The sun rose almost directly behind the mountain's peak this time of year. She thought of that and prayed the seam held.

The day dragged for her. The reports and phone calls lacked importance, relevance. She found herself trying to overhear other people, drawn to their conversations, listening to hear if anyone mentioned the tear, the flash, the lightening when there was no storm. But no one mentioned it. No one, it seemed, had noticed.

By lunch, she had exhausted the news as a source of explanation. She decided to try the experts in the field. She called the university department of astronomy.

"I, eh . . ." she was more hesitant than she wanted to be. "I thought I saw something in the sky. I was wondering . . . were there any unusual events yesterday, about six?"

"Nope. Nothing that we know about. What did you see?" The voice on the other end of the line was young and impatient.

"Ah, well, just something . . bright."

"It was probably just a weather balloon. Lots of people see those things and think they're something else. They can be quite bright when the sun hits them."

"I guess."

She hung up. Why would they tell her anything anyway? Why would they want anyone to know the sky had torn?

That evening, she did not turn to look at the peak as she drove home. It was there, though, barely visible in her peripheral vision. She could almost see it better this way, a crooked blue line and a ripple . . . like a dart in a badly made dress.

At home, she took her bowl of cereal and sat on the back porch and watched the mountain peak as the sun set behind her. As the sky grew first green, then pink, and finally violet, the seam darkened, too, until it stood out as if someone had taken a felt pen and traced it there. The sky continued to darken, but she did not go inside. She waited, watching as Orion made his appearance.

There he was. She knew it. The tear had happened right in front of him directly across his middle and now the seam of the overlapping sky was thick, too thick and Orion was missing a star from his belt.

The next day she called the university again.

"What's wrong with Orion's belt?"

"Huh?" the same young voice had answered.

"I said, what's wrong with Orion's belt? The middle star is missing."

"Hey, lady, we sure didn't notice anything here."

"Well you should have. Look tonight, just after he appears," and she hung up.

The following day she could not get through to the

University. The lines, it seems, were always busy. She continued to call all during her lunch hour until it was too late to eat. She was on her way back to her desk when she overheard two women just going on break.

"Did you hear about all that hoopla over at the University? Seems some young kid over there has discovered some sort of phenomenon, a cloud of gas or something. You can tell it's there by looking at . . . "

They were beyond hearing distance, but she didn't need to hear. She finished the sentence for them, " . . . Orion's belt."

She didn't go directly home after work that night, but instead, drove toward the mountain. It was well into sunset when she reached the scenic view turn-about at the mountains crest. People, singlely, in couples and small groups, watched from their cars and positions along the safety railing as the sun set lower and the city below began to slowly light up.

She parked her car, but did not join the others in gloating over this mixture of nature and man. Instead she turned east and made her way up the last rise of slippery shale to where she could look out across the valley on the other side.

She could see it clearly from here, a line darting down from above her head to just below her feet. It wasn't as bad as she had thought. It stopped well above the horizon and down toward the bottom, it appeared to be a much cleaner tear, almost a cut, neatly pieced together with edges matching.

But still, the edges had been badly frayed at the top and the tension it must put on the rest of the sky to stretch so the edges could overlap must be tremendous.

"It'll never hold."

She looked down toward the voice and discovered a small

girl no older than seven standing beside her. She wondered why she had not heard the girl approach on the loose rock.

"It'll never hold," the girl said again this time turning from the tear to look directly into her face.

"I don't think so either," was all she could answer.

"Susan!" The moment was broken by the clank of sliding shale and a mother's cry. Soon the mother, bent over, balancing sliding feet with fingertips gripping loose rock, emerged from the growing darkness.

"Susan! What do you think you're doing climbing up here in the dark? You could slip and break your neck or worse!"

The mother stopped short, startled by the woman she met face to face when she stood up.

"Susan!"

"It's okay, mom. I just wanted to see the sky."

"Well, the sunset's the other direction. Come on. Give me your hand. I'll help you down."

The mother grabbed her daughter by the hand, but before she could tug her down the hillside, the girl held out a clenched fist.

"Here."

She took it, an oblong strip of wrinkled paper with the ends folded over. In the darkness she could barely make it out, a Band-aid with stars on it.

Some one else knows, was all she could think about on the drive home. And if I know and she knows there have got to be others who know. And even if the experts don't know or won't tell us they know, we know and we will tell each other we know.

But who? And how would she find these others, if they did exist, or even the little girl from the mountaintop again?

That night she dreamt she went to work naked. She tried to explain to everyone how all her clothes had fallen apart, how everything she had tried on had just dissolved at the seams. She offered the explanation of how poorly made clothes were today. Everyone knew that.

She tried to cover herself up, grabbed at curtains, jackets, towels, but everything disintegrated at her touch, shredded between her fingers, cloth into threads, threads into nothing.

But what was most disturbing to her was that no one seemed to notice her nakedness or, if they did, care about it. They just went about their business as she desperately tried to hide herself.

She awoke sweating and chilled, groping for the covers that lay knotted at her feet.

She didn't drive to work that day, but took the bus instead. She suddenly felt guilty for her participation in the destruction of the environment, like a child who slips the half eaten candy bar back into its wrapper when it is discovered it was meant for the crippled boy next door.

She took a place behind the driver in one of those seats that faces the aisle. Across from her sat an older woman, her tight, white curls surrounding a face creased with stoicism. Behind the woman, through the tinted glass of the bus window, she could barely discern the shadow of the tear cutting across the glare of the morning sun.

The woman stared out the front of the bus. She wore a pale, blue suit with matching hat that bobbled amid her curls with the motion of the bus. One gloved hand grasped the top of a cane. The other hand clutched a white, lace handkerchief.

The old woman turned slowly toward her, and she watched as a gloved hand reached across the aisle and plucked a thread from the sleeve of her gabardine jacket. The old woman smiled and then turned back toward the front of the bus.

The rest of the bus now held her attention. There had been many riders when she had first gotten on. Now there were few.

There was the older gentleman in the red bow tie and bowler hat; the middle-aged woman in the dotted Swiss, a contrasting scarf sculpted around her neck. A teenaged boy, his hair slicked back and shiny, sat in the seat just behind hers. His Ramie shirt billowed about him and then neatly tucked into his designer slacks.

She looked down at her own attire, the jacket layered over matching silk blouse and pants. She looked at each of them. They might as well be going to a wedding . . . or a funeral.

The bus stopped again and the last Levi and corduroy -clad riders disembarked. Two girls, the metallic spandex molded to their not yet shapely bodies, chittered together as they boarded. Gold bobbed from their ears and jangled at their waists. They jostled their way to the seat across from the teenage boy. He swallowed hard and ran his hand over his hair. They darted their heads back and forth, whispering their commentary between giggles.

A woman in a net and ruffle formal climbed aboard after them, her broad, ruffled skirt herding a child in pink lace along in front of it. The girl's knees kicked up her skirts as she clamored up the steps.

As the mother combed change from her purse for the fare, the child settled onto the seat next to her. It was the girl from the mountaintop.

She tugged up at her socks and down at her skirt. "I

wanted to wear my coveralls like the astronauts, but mom said this'd be best."

She looked down at the girl and then reached into her pocket. The girl watched as she pulled out the wrinkled strip of stars from the night before.

The child shook her head. "I guess we won't be needing that now."

The mother situated herself next to the old woman. She reached across the aisle and patted the girl on the leg then turned toward the front window of the bus. They were a pair, the old woman in her blue suit and the mother in her formal, sitting straight-backed, knees together, heads at corresponding angles.

The bus made no other stops. The driver, her uniform crisp with creases, made a right turn at the mountain drive into the morning sun.

The girl snuggled hard against her arm. "This is it," the child said. This is it.

1992

Got cha

"So . . . this guy got into your car . . ."

Got, she thought. Like you got your gun out, got your finger on the trigger and got the bullet to fly out of the barrel and across the parking lot until it got the kid trying to out run it.

"No," she said. She spaced her words deliberately to fit the spaces in-between the skepticism he had been laying down in front of her for the last hour. "He jerked the door open, jumped in and shoved me against the driver's side of the car. Got it?" She leaned forward, trying to see behind the eyes that held her so blindly.

"Yeah, got cha. Like I said." He scrunched his lips together, scraping his mustache against the tip of his nose. "Maybe it'd be better if you talked to a female officer."

She fell back into the chair and just stared at the man. It was one of those moments when everything falls into place. An epiphany of understanding. Like the time the boulder the guy was chipping his name into had had enough and shuddered. Rolling forward, it crushed the man's leg beneath it, trapping him in the middle of nowhere until nobody found him. It was at the moment she heard the story that she understood poetic justice. Now, it was she who shuddered. And, looking at the man across from her, she understood justifiable homicide. She smiled. She chuckled. She shuddered and the laughter rumbled up and out of her.

The detective leaned forward but quickly moved back. She laughed harder. He glanced toward the open door of the interview room. The laughter thundered. She couldn't help it. Every time she looked at him, every time he made some furtive move, the laughter grew.

Tears filled her eyes and smeared the man into the wall behind him. She got up and went to the door, grabbing the frame half for support. She looked back at him and roared. Her sides ached and she gasped for breath. She could hardly get the words out. "Gotta go. If you think of anything else, call me. Got it?"

The detective sputtered, but couldn't get any words out. She threw her head back and the sound that spewed from her drowned the rest of the station to silence. A woman in uniform started toward her, but was stopped by a gesture directed at the detective still standing at the far side of the interview room and the words, "Don't bother. We got it."

The laughter continued as she limped toward the exit, supporting herself on the shoulder of the female officer as she passed. It was the door swinging closed behind her that finally quelled the turbulence. Though the outburst subsided, her body continued to shudder. Now, it was with cold. She folded her arms tight across her chest and made her way to the parking lot and sunlight.

She stood next to her car. The sun on her back warmed her, but still she did not open the door. She fiddled with the keys, dropped them, picked them up and fiddled some more. Finally, she unlocked the door and opened it.

The smell that tumbled out pushed her back. It was him. Cigarette smoke and tainted breath. The heavy pungency of grease and sweat. Hot breath against her neck. Unshaven. Rough. Nails scratching her arm.

She got in, closed the door and quickly rolled the window down, leaned across to roll down the widow on the opposite side, but stopped. She checked the door lock instead, sat up straight, and tried to breathe.

The wind blew across her as she drove down the freeway, but could not push the stench from her nostrils. Finally home, she hurried up the steps and locked the door of the apartment behind her. She leaned over the kitchen sink and threw water on her face, gagged and barely made it to the toilet before vomiting.

"How do you know he wanted to rape you?" "Did you see a knife?" "Maybe he just wanted a ride." "Did he say he was going to kill you?"

The detective's questions pummeled her mind as she played back the day piece by piece. She argued with them. Refuted them. Found herself siding with them and adding her own. Nothing really happened. She didn't see a knife. He didn't actually hurt her. Maybe it was a pen in his coat pocket. If she had given him a ride to where he wanted to go, maybe he would of just gotten out.

She opened the closet door and stood before the full-length mirror. She hesitated, toyed with just closing the door and leaving it alone; with turning her back on the image before her and embracing the detective who still hounded at her back. She smoothed the wrinkles from her sweater then lifted its hem and pulled the blouse from her slacks.

The line. Small. Maybe a quarter of an inch. Parallel to her ribs. Red. Dry now, with a smear crusted around it. She touched it, rubbed it, pushed hard against it until blood oozed free, staining her fingertips. She lowered her blouse and sunk onto the edge of the bed.

She thought of the man in the car, felt the knife against her side. Saw the detective, eyes probing, words digging, penetrating her every thought. He pulled at her, pushed at her, pressed in on her. She shoved back. He struggled. She squeezed, clasping sweater and flesh until the wound stung. Then, wrapping her fingers tight around her side, she smiled.

"Got cha."

Saving Grace

Gracie stared at the rust-colored water, slowly clearing as the sand settled out of it and into the bottom the old cast iron tub. She shifted uncomfortably in her so-called robes. The white curtains with the pale pink roses hung as limply from her shoulders as they had from the rod in the bedroom from which they had been borrowed.

"You sure this is gonna work?"

"Why wouldn't it?"

"'Cause this ain't no church and you ain't no preacher."

"I'm a preacher's daughter and anyway, church is anywhere two or more gather in His name."

"I ain't heard His name yet."

"You will. Now are you going to get in or not?"

It had taken them three days to push, pull, haul and finally roll the old tub down the hill and out of sight of the house and Gracie wasn't about to back out now. She and Jen had a pact; no matter what, they were going to stick together. Wherever one of them went, the other was going to go too, and even though Gracie didn't mind the idea of going to Hell, Jen sure didn't want to go. 'My daddy would kill me if I ended up in Hell,' she had said when she found out Gracie had never been baptized. 'You got to get saved, Gracie.' Gracie stepped over the rim of the tub and into the water.

"Damn! It's cold!"

"It's creek water. Of course it's cold. And you shouldn't be cussing in the Lord's house."

"Well, do you think the Lord would of minded if we had heated it up a bit?"

"You're not going to be in it that long, so just sit down and be quiet."

The bottom of the curtain tangled itself around Gracie's legs. She stood tugging at it and squirming against the string that held it tight around her waist.

"I don't know why I have to wear this thing just to get baptized."

"Because that's the way it's done. You're supposed to wear white robes, like Jesus and John the Baptist did. He was the first one to baptize people.

"I bet he didn't use an old bath tub."

"No. He used the river. You want to go down to the river and let me baptize you there? Because, if that's what you want, we can do it. Right now. Let's go." Jen stood up, ready to stomp off to the river and throw Gracie to the currents.

"You know I can't swim."

"Then shut your mouth and sit down. I can't dunk you if you're standing up."

Gracie eased down into the water grimacing as the cold inched its way up her body.

"Whatever happened to that John guy?"

"John the Baptist? They cut off his head for talking too

much. Okay, now. Just relax."

Jen knelt down next to the tub. She put one hand on the back of Gracie's head and pressed the other against her forehead.

"Do you believe the Holy Father sent his one and only begotten son, Jesus Christ, to die for your sins?"

"I guess so."

Jen released her hold on Gracie's head and sat back on her haunches. "You can't just guess so. You have to know so. This is serious, Gracie. Now do you believe or not?"

"How am I suppose to know if I believe if I ain't never seen God or Jesus or anything else?"

"But that's the idea of believing. If you knew for sure then there wouldn't be any reason to believe because you'd know and believing means you don't know but you're still going to go along with it anyway."

"Yeah?"

"Yeah."

"Okay, then. I guess I believe."

Jen's eyes narrowed.

"I mean, I believe, all right? Yeah, I believe. Sure. If that's what believing means then I for sure believe I believe. Now, can we get this over with? I'm about to freeze my bageezes off."

Jen put her hand behind Gracie's head, pinched Gracie's nose harder than she needed to and tilted her head back. Gracie grabbed for air, puffing her cheeks out and squinting her eyes shut as Jen pushed her down under the water. Jen took her time, clearing her throat and molding her impatience into pious calm. The knuckles gripping the sides of the tub blanched white.

"Then . . . in the name of the Father, the Son and the Holy Ghost," her voice took on the tremor of a sermon. "I wash you clean of all your sins . . . and welcome you . . . into the fold . . . of our Lord and Savior . . . Je-sus Christ. Amen"

Gracie flew upright, water spewing as she gasped for breath.

"Jesus! I didn't know you was gonna drown me! I thought the whole idea was to save me. Save me so I could get to heaven with you! Not kill me so I could get there first!"

"You're not dead. Didn't come anywhere near dying. Just suffered a little, like He did for your damn near rotten soul."

Gracie's mouth dropped open and she stared at Jen.

"You just swore."

Jen blushed.

"And right here in church, too."

"This isn't a church."

"Yes it is. You said so. 'Anywhere two or more get together in His name.' That's what you said, and that makes this a church and that means you swore in God's house."

Jen sat back on her heels, biting her lip. It was the look Gracie hated to see and never knew quite for sure what to do when she saw it. A tear welled up in the corner of Jen's eye and started down her cheek. Gracie wiped it away with a wet hand.

"Shit, Jen. I'm sorry."

"That doesn't mean you can go on and start cussing, Gracie."

"I got to do something. I don't want to end up in heaven if you're endin' up in hell."

"I'm not going to hell and neither are you. We're saved, Gracie. And whether you like it or not, once you're saved it's forever, unless you take it all back, which you're not going to do. Now get out of that tub. Your lips are darn near blue."

The fire they built nibbled at the stick Gracie teased it with. Jen pushed more of the log into the flames then gathered the curtains from the rock where they had been drying. Gracie thrust her stick saber-like at the coals.

"Jen?"

"Yeah."

"Did you feel any different? I mean, after you got saved?"

"My daddy says baptizing us was just a formality because we were born saved, being he's a preacher and all." She wrapped the curtains around Gracie's shoulders.

"How do you know if it takes?"

"It always takes."

"But how do you know?"

Jen settled down on the log next to Gracie. "My daddy's baptized hundreds of people and none of them ever came back to do it again. I mean, some of them probably ended up with the devil in them, but that's because they took it back, what was said when they were baptized."

Gracie pulled the curtains tighter around her shoulders. Even with dry clothes on she was still cold.

"The devil, huh?"

"Yeah."

"Jen?"

"Yeah?"

"About what you said at the tub. You never told me about no ghosts before."

Jen pushed in closer to Gracie. "That's okay. There's only one."

Indigo

In her dreams she was indigo. Not named for the color, but the color itself. It was she who touched the sky and sent a diffusion of darkness spreading from its eastern edge to the west. The one who placed the layer of depth beneath the water. The rich luster at the bottom of the sapphire. The illusion of blackness floating in the night. Indigo. Rich, deep, cool. Far removed from the reality of the day.

In her dreams there was no scorching white, no blood red. No orange to cause pain. No green to gag upon. She was the other end of the spectrum. The abyss. The serenity. The opulence.

The alarm blared and she slammed her hand down on it. It was only three a.m. but the glare through the window pierced her eyes, and she squinted hard against it. Time had not been adjusted to account for the longer days. It was like some unfounded act of hope to continue the clocks as they had always been. Instead, life had adjusted around the pseudo reality of time. Work, for now, started at five a.m. and lasted until nine p.m. The four-hour break in the middle in addition to the two lunch breaks was somehow to make the schedule tolerable. Tomorrow, at least tomorrow so to speak, work would start at five p.m. and go until nine the next morning. It didn't quite fit the thirty-five hour rotation but was easy to remember. It would be this way for at least another two months, if there weren't any more major changes.

It was the night rotation she liked to work best. Then, in her mind at least, she could live her dream. Wrapped in sweet darkness, she could touch the sky, brush the waters and relish in their richness. The brightness, she no longer liked calling it day, was then the time to sleep and in her dreams she didn't simply avoid the light, she nullified it. It amazed and reassured her that she could sleep almost twenty-four hours without waking and in doing so escape facing the sun on those rotations.

She slipped the baseball cap on, its exaggerated bill extending far beyond her nose, and pulled the hood of the white windbreaker up over the top of it. The gloves she secured under the elastic at her wrists. Her slacks were long enough that she didn't need to tuck them into her socks. Even when she sat, her legs were well covered. She refused to take a change of clothing. Her coworkers chided her for giving in. Once inside the building, they wore the clothes they always had, short skirts, tank tops, sleeves rolled up to reveal bare arms. She saw them as delusional. For some reason they had not yet understood the meaning of the light. They either had not yet felt the pain as it stabbed into their daily existence or had some how developed a way to ignore it.

She couldn't ignore it. She understood too clearly what it meant. She had refused to be blinded by the explanations and resolutions that had been proffered by the experts. "The slowing was slowing." "Change was possible." "Life would continue."

She knew, in the end, only the shadow people would survive. Only those, who by the luck of the spin ended up in the confines where light meets night and twilight and dusk are unrelenting, would be able to endure. As the wheel slowed, the ball would settle and the domain would be chosen. And there, in narrow strips banished to opposite sides of the orb, indigo would be the constant across the sky.

The Good Side

It was the weight of that arm she missed just now. It wasn't always the same. Sometimes it was her shoes scattered in the middle of the floor or finding the toothpaste left uncapped. But just now, it was that arm, draped across her waist in the abandon of sleep that she missed.

It hadn't always been that way. At first it had been uncomfortable, waking to that arm heavy across her. You're on my side, she would tell her. Because it's the good side, would be the reply.

Later, after they had grown tired of each other, she would push the arm off only to have it find its way back. Do you have to do that, she would demand. And will you leave if I do, came the rebuttal.

They never quite reached exhaustion, or perhaps they did. In either case, neither had the desire, let alone the strength, to leave.

They became used to each other. She came to expect the milk carton unclosed and the cupboard left ajar, the newspaper folded back to the crossword half done.

And that arm, clammy in summer, warm in winter, nestled in the crevice just above her hip, reaching for the good side of the bed.

1997

Aunt Jessie

The tree it had fallen from stood taller than the old school house the oak stood behind. I knew the best thing to do was to find its nest and return it. The old tale about a mother bird not taking her young back after it had been touched by human hands just wasn't true. But that oak stood massive, and if I had searched all day I might not find the nest let alone be able to reach it. Anyway, I wanted that bird and being already late was just the excuse I needed.

I carefully cradled it in my hand and slipped it beneath my jacket, then hurried the rest of the way to Jessie's house.

I knew she'd be in the kitchen, slamming food on the stove and keeping one ear cocked to hear me come in. Aunt Jessie hadn't wanted any children. She made that clear the day I showed up on her front porch, suitcase in hand.

"You're family and you ain't got nobody else so I guess I'm stuck."

I didn't want Aunt Jessie either. I was her brother's only child–the daughter he had hoped would be a son–the daughter of a brother she had never liked.

"I'm only doin' this 'cause you're blood . . . and for your mama. Remember that."

"You're late."

I stood in the mud-room out of sight, but the squeak of the screen door had given me away.

"Yes, Ma'am. I came by the old school house." I tried to make my stride as natural as possible. Maybe I could slip through the kitchen. Maybe she'd think I had homework or something I had to do.

"Hold it right there, Missy. What you got?"

"Nothing." I started to keep on walking, but her voice stopped me.

"Under your coat. What you got there?"

"Nothing, Aunt Jessie."

"Don't nothin' me, Missy. Now show me what you got under your coat, or do I have to jerk it off ya?"

I opened my jacket and slowly pulled my hand out. Rolled into a ball was a mass of feathers matted together by the sweat of my palm.

Jessie clicked her tongue that way she did when things disgusted her. "It's just gonna die, you know. You better give it to me."

My hand jerked back instinctively.

"Give it to me, I said."

She stretched out her hand, her long, bony fingers pointing at me. I cradled the bird with both hands against my chest.

"What do you think I'm going to do, wring it's neck?'

I did. I thought of all those chickens I had to catch for her. Running them down, cornering them in the coop, grabbing them any way I could, their wings beating furiously against my arms, my chest, my face. I'd fight back the tears as I handed them to her. She'd grab them by the legs and in one

94

fluid motion swing them down onto the block and the axe onto their necks.

I tilted my hand and the struggling bird slipped into hers.

It seemed like a long time that we stood there like that. Me with my hand still out-stretched. Aunt Jessie looking at the bird as it raised its head then fell forward from the weight of it.

"You think I'm gonna hold this thing all day? Go git a box, an' don't make it no huge one either. An' that ol' quilt you drug out to the barn, pull some stuffin' out of it to put in it."

I didn't move.

"Git, I said."

I turned and ran from the kitchen. From under the dresser I dragged the shoebox that held every treasure I had. I untied the lid and dumped the contents onto the bed, then ran back through the kitchen.

"Don't slam that...."

I caught the door with my hand, then tore for the barn. I pushed the soft cotton batting I pulled from the quilt into the shape of a nest as best I could and hurried the box back to the kitchen.

Aunt Jessie slipped the bird into the nest.

"You gotta put a light on this thing or it'll freeze. Here," she handed me a dishcloth. "Tie this around that lamp on the desk up there so it won't be too hot. And you gotta feed it. It looks like nothin' but a mocking bird. Grubs would be best, but I guess worms will do, but not from my garden. Now git that dirty thing out of here. I got supper to fix."

It seemed to take Jessie a long time before she got supper

ready that day. By the time she called me to the table I had the bird set up on the desk and had dug some worms from behind the chicken coop. We sat at the table eating, only the sound of the old ceiling fan between us.

"I put the light on the bird just like you said to, Aunt Jessie."

She took a piece of corn bread and slipped butter between its halves.

"I hope I did it right. And I dug up some worms..."

"You put the shovel back?"

"Yes, ma'am, back in the shed. But he wouldn't eat so I don't think he's hungry yet."

She took my plate to the stove and refilled it.

"If it ain't hungry, it'll be dead."

"I tried to give him the worm. I held it up to him and everything."

She sat down and handed my plate back to me.

"Could . . . could you come up and see if I did everything right? Please?"

She buttered another piece of corn bread and put it on the edge of my plate.

"I'll see."

I was sitting at the desk watching the chest of the bird rise and fall when Jessie entered. She didn't say anything, just slipped her hand in between the bird and the light then adjusted the neck of the lamp so it was a little further away from the box. She then pulled a pair of tweezers from the pocket of her dress.

"Git me a worm."

I fished three out of the can. With the tweezers, she picked up the smallest one, bent over the box and began stroking the bird under its beak with the food. I was so intent on watching her that it was a while before I realized that she was cooing to the bird, too. In soft murmured tones she clucked and cooed and clicked as she gently stroked the bird.

Suddenly, the bird's head lifted, its beak opened, and Aunt Jessie slipped the worm, tweezers and all, into it's throat. "Git me another worm."

I held out my hand and she picked up the next worm. This time she barely touched the bird's beak before it opened to receive the food. I gave Jessie the last worm and dug into the can for more.

"No more. Stuffed bird's same as a starved one. You gotta feed that thing a little, but you gotta feed it often. You feed it the last thing before you go to bed and the first thing when you git up in the morning."

"What about school?"

"You feed it whenever you can."

She set the tweezers on the desk and turned to leave.

"What's that mess on the bed?"

"It was in the box. I had to dump it out. It's okay, I'll find some place for it."

Jessie stood over the bed and looked down at the treasures that had once been safely hidden under the dresser. In amongst the stones and sea shells, the costume jewelry and Cracker Jack toys was all I had left of my parents, a cluster of things gathered in haste and set aside for a time when remembering would come easier. There were a few photographs from one of our vacations, the letters my mother had written to me at camp last summer, my father's fountain pen and the necklace my mother always wore on special occasions because it made her feel "special."

Aunt Jessie reached down and with one long finger shifted things out of the way of the photographs. Her finger paused over one. It was from the time we went to the beach, a picture of Mama, her hair blown back and she's laughing. Then Jessie's finger found the necklace. She followed the chain until she came to the locket. She picked it up and rubbed it between her thumb and finger. She didn't really look at it, just held it for a while then let it drop back onto the bed.

"Don't leave no mess." And she was gone.

The next three days of school were agony. Sitting, squirming, waiting for the last bell to ring, all I could think about was a tiny bird, mouth gaping, begging for food with no one there to give it any.

"Don't slam the..."

I caught the door with my hand and ran through the kitchen.

"Hi, Aunt Jessie," I called as I hurried toward the incessant chirping.

The bird sat on the edge of the nest, gray feathers poking through white down. He cocked his head to watch me. I got the can of worms and began digging through the desk drawer for the tweezers.

"That can's almost empty." Jessie stood in the doorway. "If you're gonna keep that thing fed you're gonna have to keep that can full."

"Yes, Ma'am."

She pulled the tweezers from her pocket and set them on the desk. The bird eyed her, made an awkward lunge toward her and slid from its perch.

"You're gonna need a bigger box pretty soon, too. Don't want that thing flyin' around and messing up the place."

"I could get one from the grocery store."

Jessie nodded. The bird pushed itself against the side of the box, wings flapping, as if trying to find a way through the cardboard wall to the woman standing there. Jessie walked to the window and the bird fluttered along in its box following her movement. She fingered a piece of wallpaper that was peeling away from the window casing. Darker patches on the wall where pictures had once hung revealed that the paper had once been blue. Even then it had most likely clashed with the now worn green linoleum on the floor.

Jessie looked around the room: The desk, a chair, a dresser and nightstand, the metal trundle bed I slept on in the corner. I had only recently discovered how to pull the mass of metal from beneath it to reveal its hidden mattress. It now hid the treasures that had once filled the shoebox.

"I guess this room's okay. Not much use anymore, not now." She hesitated, rubbing the paint chips still clinging to the bed frame. "Your mother used to use it."

She turned to leave. Then, just for an instant, she rested her hand on my shoulder. It was the first time Aunt Jessie and I had ever touched.

It was Saturday. The bird, his belly full, sat sleeping in his makeshift nest. I tried to pull my corduroy overalls on quietly, but with each rustle of clothing the bird's feathers quivered. I picked up my shoes and tiptoed stocking-footed out of the room.

Jessie was dishing eggs onto my plate and stacking toast on the side when I reached the kitchen.

"Bird's fed," I said as I slipped my shoes on and tied the laces. "My bed's made, too, and as soon as I'm finished with breakfast, I'm going to start cleaning out the shed like you've been wanting me to."

Jessie handed me a glass of milk then stood staring at me from across the table. I turned to my plate of eggs.

"I know I've been putting the shed off, but I'm going to get it done. I promise."

"Those overalls . . . they're gittin' kind of small for you, ain't they?"

"They're okay, Aunt Jessie. I've been taking real good care of them."

"Stand up."

I stood. Jessie stepped around the table. Three inches of white sock glared between the bottom of my pant legs and my shoes. I had extended the straps on the overalls as far as they would go, but they still pulled hard on the buttons. Jessie reached down and barely touched her fingertips to the cloth worn thin at the knees. She stood up quickly.

"Finish your eggs or they'll be cold. I thought we'd go down to McClosson's. Maybe see about gittin' you some new pants, maybe something nice for school, maybe some shoes."

The last bite never made it to my mouth. My fork drifted back to the plate, and I sat there, mouth still open awaiting its arrival. Jessie looked at me.

"Well, do you want to go or not?"

"Yes, Ma'am!" I jumped up and hurried to the sink to wash my plate.

We didn't talk the entire drive into town. I sat on the edge of the front seat watching the gravel road in front of us as it came and went. I turned my head a little, just far enough to see Jessie out of the corner of my eye. She sat up straight behind the wheel of the Buick, eyes never veering from the road, her hair, as always, pulled back into a tight bun. I studied the sharp outline of her profile, trying to find somewhere in her features some reminder of my father, some resemblance to his broad grin and narrow brow that had always seemed creased with laughter. I couldn't find any. Jessie's face was long and narrow. Her eyes were deep set, dark and they didn't sparkle when she spoke. The lines that creased her brow and trailed from the corners of her eyes were not put there by laughter or even bemusement, but had come, it seemed, from repeated disappointment and displeasure.

We pulled into the parking lot at McClosson's. I hurried to keep up with Jessie as I followed her inside.

"Find some things. Let's see what fits," was all she said.

She stood outside the dressing room as I tried things on. I would step out from behind the curtain and turn around in front of her. She would nod once or give a shake of her head to indicate what she thought about the fit or style. Sometimes she would just look, her brow knitted together, then shrug her shoulders.

In the shoe department, she told me to stand, walk and raise up on my toes while she bent down and poked at the toe of the shoe and tried to slip her fingers in at the heel. She wrapped socks around my fist and had the woman at the counter find underwear to fit me. By the time we headed for the door, I carried four bags full. I had three pairs of pants, four shirts, a week's worth of socks and underwear, a good dress and a new pair of tennis shoes.

"Why, Jessie."

The man's voice stopped her just short of the door.

"Haven't seen you in here for a while. And who might this be? Your niece? Tom and Addie's girl? Why, ain't she a pretty one. I'd heard she had come to live with you after the accident last summer."

Jessie wanted to leave, I could tell that. I knew she didn't like being around people. She made sure I went to church every Sunday but never went herself. And she had never gone to anything at school. She even phoned in her grocery order and had it delivered to the house or had me run in to pick it up.

"Sorry about Tom." The man kept talking. "I'd have come to the funeral, but it was the middle of our summer clearance sale and I just couldn't get away. Don't know why they were laid to rest all the way up in Oaksdale, anyway."

I looked at Jessie. I could see her jaw getting tight and could hear the skillet slamming on the stove back at the house.

"Aunt Jessie, can we go now? Please? I really have to use the bathroom."

Jessie looked down at me then back to the man. "Clint."

"Jessie. Nice talking to you. Now hurry back, you hear? And I am sorry about Tom and Addie."

Jessie drove the Buick to the end of the block and pulled into the gas station. She drove past the pumps and parked at the side of the building.

"Well?"

I looked at her.

"You have to use the bathroom?"

I looked down at the floor in front of me. I could feel my ears grow hot as my face reddened. Jessie started the car and headed toward the house.

"You know you ain't supposed to lie."

"Yes, Ma'am."

I tried to look at Jessie without looking up. I wanted to

see just how mad she was, at the man for talking to her and at me for lying. But all I could see were her hands, those long, knotted fingers gripping the steering wheel. All but one. One finger seemed to be keeping time to some song I couldn't hear, tapping the rhythm lightly on the wheel. I listened closely. It was there, barely audible above the rumble of the gravel beneath the tires of the car, a tune I didn't recognize. Aunt Jessie was humming.

It took the rest of Saturday and most of Sunday afternoon to get the shed clean. In between dangling worms in front of the bird, I sorted canning jars by size, threw out old magazines and made a pile of tools without handles and handles without tools. I swept out cobwebs and dust and did my best to repair crumbling shelves. I tossed out rusted cans and parts of automobiles that were no longer identifiable. By Sunday afternoon, I had reached the last obstacle . . . an old saddle slung over a trunk.

Through the dust, the saddle looked black, although I knew it had most likely been brown. The leather, once shiny, was now dull and brittle and the horn had turned green with tarnish. It was heavier than I thought, but I managed to lift the saddle and set it to one side.

I couldn't undo the catch on the trunk, but the hinges had rusted through, and I got the lid open. Most of the clothes and books inside had been gnawed on or nibbled through by mice and everything was so old it seemed to crumble in my hands. There were books of poems and the complete works of different people. There were cowboy shirts and skirts and a dress that had layer after layer of green netting. And there was a box.

The box was metal with a picture of a herd of buffalo

embossed on the lid. I tried prying the lid off with my fingers, but it was too tight and I tore a fingernail instead. I shook the box. Inside I could hear the contents as they slid with each shake and knocked against the ends.

I set the box to one side and put everything else back in the trunk. I replaced the saddle, gave the shed a final sweep and carried the last of the tin cans and paper out to the trash barrels. Then, slipping the box into my overalls, I headed for the house.

The bird was chirping for his supper when I reached the back door. Jessie sat in her rocking chair on the front porch. I was sure she could hear the bird, and I wondered why she hadn't hollered at me to come feed it. I hurried upstairs and dug some worms from the can.

The bird no longer had to be coaxed into eating. He opened his beak readily for each worm and anything else he thought might possibly be one. I held him in my hand, his claws clasped around my finger. He seemed more feathers than down now and he would open up his wings and beat them against the air as he still held tight to my hand. I knew it wouldn't be long before he would be trying to fly, and I still hadn't gotten the box Jessie had told me to get.

Once fed, the bird settled on the edge of his nest and I settled on the bed with the tin box. It took a while, but by inching corner after corner I was finally able to pry the lid off. The contents spilled onto the bed. They were pictures. A mound of photographs of horses and more horses and some people. As I looked at them, I started to sort them into piles without really thinking about it. There was a pile for the big red horse and one for the white one with the cream-colored mane and tail. And another pile of the two of them together.

I made a pile for bunches of horses together, one for people and horses and another of just people.

When I recognized the old barn, I knew these horses had once been a part of Aunt Jessie's place. The pictures had to have been taken a long time ago, though. The doors on the barn hung straight and the fence around the corral had all its railings.

I started back through the photographs to see if I could find my father among the people in them. I scrutinized the figures in each picture, but it wasn't my father's face I found. It was Mama's. In picture after picture, there was my mother, her hair blown back, riding horses, standing beside them, sitting on top of fences, her face always full of laughter. Then I looked closer at the other person who was in almost every picture with Mama. A tall, thin woman, her hair hanging to her waist, and with long thin fingers that wrapped around my mother's waist or held her by the shoulders. A woman whose narrow face also was filled with laughter.

"Missy!"

I quickly put the pictures back into the box and slid it between the mattress and the trundle bed beneath.

Jessie was still on the porch. She had a large bowl in her lap and was reaching into a bag beside her chair and coming up with handfuls of snap beans. She nodded toward the metal lawn chair, and I pulled it up to the bag and reached in for a fist full. I popped off the tips on each bean then snapped them into pieces.

"You get that bird fed?"

"Yes, Ma'am."

"He sit on your hand?"

I nodded.

"There was some grubs in my garden. They're in a jar in the mud-room. Not too short, now."

I watched her hands and gauged my pieces of snap beans to hers.

"I finished the shed."

"You got everything put back and the trash thrown out?"

"Yes, Ma'am."

She nodded and continued snapping beans.

"There was a saddle in the shed," I said.

Jessie reached for another handful of beans.

"Did you used to have horses, Aunt Jessie?"

"Used to."

"Did you ride?"

"No use having horses if you ain't gonna ride them"

"Did my daddy ride?"

"Your daddy was a business man. The only use he had for horses was if they made money."

"Did my Mama ride?"

Jessie's hands stopped and fell into the bowl in her lap. She sat silent, looking straight ahead. I waited a while before I asked again.

"Did she, Aunt Jessie?"

"Yes, Missy, your mama rode."

Her voice snapped with the beans.

"What happened to the horses?"

"They died, Missy. They died just like everything dies."

She stood up abruptly and shoved the bowl at me to throw in my last beans then disappeared into the house.

Things were different for the next couple of weeks. Jessie would ask me about school and nod when I showed her my

106

papers, and the jar of grubs on the back porch never ran empty.

In my rush to get home and feed the bird every day, I never made it to the grocer's to get a bigger box. One day when I came home from school, I discovered the shoebox and bird inside two paper bags that had been taped together to make a larger enclosure. Jessie never said a word except, "It needs a bigger box."

Then we had a cold snap. Spring disappeared and it turned cold and rainy. I would trudge home from school and stand in the mudroom pulling off my coat and boots, the bird all the time hollering at me to hurry. It was more than a week before it warmed up again.

"Aunt Jessie? I got a box. There were some at school, and Miss Sample said I could have one."

I caught the screen door with my foot and slid the box with my books inside onto the washing machine. The sound of the skillet slamming against the top of the stove paralyzed me. A few seconds later, I edged my way to the kitchen door.

Jessie stood at the counter, her back to me. She flung open the cupboard, jerked the box of corn meal out of it then slammed the door shut. She swung around toward the refrigerator, but stopped short when she saw me.

I stared back at her, caught in her glare. In the silence between us I realized the quiet of the house. No chirping called to me from the bedroom above. I ran for the stairs.

"I told you it was just gonna die, didn't I?" I raced to beat Jessie's words to the bedroom door, but they rushed past me. "I told you! I told you that!"

I reached the desk, breathless. There, in the bottom of the shoebox, lay the crumpled mound of feathers. Its beak gaped open. One eye stared at me from beneath a half closed lid. I touched its body. It was cold. I slipped my finger into its curved claws but they did not grip back. I lifted its head, but it only slid back into its death curl.

"Didn't I tell you it was just gonna to die?"

Jessie filled the doorway.

"Didn't I tell you not to bring that dirty thing in here, that it was just gonna die? Well, now you know. Everything dies!"

And she was gone.

I was still trying to catch my breath, but couldn't. I kept grabbing for more air, but couldn't find any. I wanted to yell at Jessie to come back, that I couldn't breathe, that I was going to die, too, but there was no air and there were no words. I laid on the bed and buried my face into the pillow.

When I awoke, my pillow was wet and my hair was stuck to the sides of my face. It was way past supper. I washed my face with cold water, brushed my hair back and went down to the kitchen. My place was set with a plate covered by another plate. The counters and the rest of the table were cleared. Jessie was nowhere in sight. I left the food where it was and went back upstairs.

I dug the metal box with the buffalo on it out from under the trundle bed and dumped the pictures out. I lined the box carefully with tissue then laid the bird inside and snapped the lid shut. There was still no sign of Jessie as I got the shovel from the shed and headed down the road.

It was near dark when I got to the old school house and the tree behind it cast deep shadows across its empty window frames. I buried the bird beneath the tree.

By the time I got back, the yard light filled the area

behind the house with a blue-white glow. I stood just outside the light's reach in the shadowed edge between the barn and the shed. The chickens rustled in their coop nearby and somewhere a mockingbird feigned the songs of other birds. The house sat silent.

I followed the edge of the light to the barn and slipped between the half opened doors. In the darkness, I could barely make out the stalls that lined each side. I sat down next to the wall of the first stall and stared at the screen door on the other side of the circle of light.

It was late morning when I woke up. The old quilt was heavy and hard to pull off. I felt stiff, clumsy as I stood up. My hands and feet felt heavy, and it was hard to brush the straw off my clothes and pull it out of my hair. The walk across the yard took forever.

The screen door creaked and I waited just inside, listening for Jessie. She was at the sink; the water was running.

I crept into the kitchen.

"You missed breakfast." Her voice was quiet, muffled by the water and the fan overhead. She didn't turn around.

"Sorry."

"There's corn bread and jam on the table."

The sound of the chair against the floor grated through the silence and I sat down. She set a plate and knife in front of me, then poured a glass of cold milk.

I sliced the corn bread and spread the halves with a thin layer of jam.

Jessie stood facing the window over the sink, nervously wiping her hands on her apron, wringing her long fingers in the cloth. I was hungrier than I wanted to be and was soon on my second piece of corn bread.

Jessie sat down next to me. From the pocket of her apron she brought out a stack of photographs and set them on the table between us. I froze. I slowly slipped my hands into my lap, bowed my head and waited. Only silence followed.

I glanced sideways at Jessie. She sat still working her fingers hard. I followed her gaze to the stack of photographs.

"The white one was your mother's." The photo was of two horses in the corral with two women leaning on the railings in front of them. "She called him Lightning."

"That's her on the right. She was good, real good, more than just a rider. She could really work them, train them. A lot better than me. That's me next to her. My horse is the roan."

Jessie slid the top picture from the stack.

"That's your mother on Midnight. He was just about the toughest horse we ever had, but your mother could ride him. She had no trouble with him at all. Fact is, a lot of people asked your mother to help with their horses, she was that good."

"That's me and your mother on Big Red and Lightning." We were down to the third picture. "That saddle I'm on, that's the one you found in the shed. Your mother gave that to me for Christmas."

Jessie's hands went nervously from wringing in front of her to the stack of photographs between us. As each picture was uncovered, it was accompanied by a brief narrative that barely described the occupants of the frame and rarely mentioned the events behind it. I sat motionless, staring at each picture, trying to take in each word, each phrase, each name of each horse before she moved on to the next.

"This was the last rodeo your mother rode in," she had reached the last photograph. "She won it, too. See that ribbon on the saddle?"

I nodded. Jessie pushed the last photograph toward the rest and started to get up.

"Aunt Jessie, what happened the horses?"

Jessie sighed and leaned heavily back into the chair.

"Some things just die, Missy. People die . . . birds die . . . things die."

"Did the ranch die?"

Jessie nodded. "Yes, Missy, the ranch died." She stood up and left the kitchen.

I gathered the photographs and carried them upstairs. The bed would not easily release its hidden mattress, but with tugging it finally slid out, and I looked at my treasures. I sorted out the cute things and oddities until I had the keepsakes of my life together. I went back through the photographs of the ranch and my vacation pictures. I re-read the letters my mother had written to me at camp. And then I opened the locket.

I had always thought my mother carried pictures of herself and my father in the locket, and on one side I found a photo of her at about the same age as the old photographs of the horses. But on the other side, it was Jessie's face I saw.

I found Jessie in the garden by the corral tying the limbs of tomato plants to stakes she had driven into the ground. I stooped down between the rows and began checking leaves for caterpillars, peeling them off whenever I found one and tossing their rolled bodies to the chickens scattered about.

"Be sure to check under the leaves."

"Yes, ma'am." I tossed another caterpillar to a hen. "Aunt Jessie?"

"What?"

"You think I could learn to ride a horse?"

Jessie tore a strip from an old sheet and tied up another limb.

"I ain't got no horses to ride." Her hammer drove the stake in deeper.

"I bet I could learn. Not as good as Mama, but I bet I could. Aunt Jessie?"

"What."

"That old barn sure needs to be cleaned out, doesn't it? Sure couldn't keep any horses in it like it is, even if you did have any."

Jessie finished the branch she was tying and stood up. The breeze caught loose strands of her hair and swept them across her face. She tried in vain to comb them back with her long fingers. I stood up and shoved my hands deep into the pockets of my new jeans.

"I think I'll clean out that barn this summer. Yep, I think that's what I'll do. Clean out that old barn and maybe learn to ride."

Babe

Molasses. Momma always said I moved like molasses. But that's 'cause she never saw me bubblin' inside.

"Babe!"

The tree held me tight.

"Babe! I knows you up there. You better git in this house . . . now!"

I let one foot dangle and slid the other down the trunk of the tree 'til it caught on the knot just below where the limbs forked.

"Babe! If you don't git in this house right now, you'll have your butt to pay!"

I waited. Let the rough bark imprint me cheek as I hugged my body against it. Waited, 'til I heard the screen door slam, then slid the rest of the way down the tree, my oxfords chippin' bark as they went.

Momma scooped the dishes off the table and dumped them on the counter. I pushed the screen door open just enough to make the hinges squeak. Momma didn't bother to look at me. Just snatched the forks off the kitchen table and clanked the glasses together in her hand.

"Sometimes, Babe, I just don't know what to do with you. Why is it I've always got to holler before you come?" She tossed the silverware into the sink.

I opened the cupboard and dug past the worn-out underwear that topped the rag bag, looking for something of decent size.

Momma pushed past me. She rammed her arm into the bag up to her elbow and pulled out an old tee-shirt. Socks and panties tumbled out with it. She grabbed them up and crammed them back into the bag then shoved the tee-shirt at me.

"Here. Now git in there and git busy, would ya'."

She swept the last few dishes into the sink and turned the water on full blast. Suds bubbled up and over the plates and things.

"Babe!"

Mama's like water on a hot skillet. She can't stay still. Never could. She's always got to be jumpin' from one thing to me and back again. She flipped the water off and wiped her hands dry.

"I gotta be gittin' to town, but you can take care of this, can't you?"

This meant the whole house. She grabbed up her pocketbook, and I trailed after her to the bathroom.

"I won't be long." She painted her lips bright red then scrubbed the stuff off her teeth with her finger. "An' I'm bringin' company back so I want the place to look nice."

She squeezed by me and into the bedroom.

"Who?" I asked.

Momma pulled her flowered shirtwaist out of the closet

and held it to her. "You like this?"

I nodded.

"I don't know. Maybe your daddy." She winked. She tugged her sweater off then let the shirtwaist slide down her arms and over her head.

"Now don't go wastin' time." She squinted into the broken mirror over the dresser, pushed her hair into place with her fingers, then spun around to me. "How do I look?"

I shrugged. "Fine, I guess."

"I don't want you lolly gaggin' around. I'm not gonna be too late, now." She grabbed a sweater and squeezed by me and down the hall, stopping at the kitchen door. "Sometimes, Babe, I swear, you move just like molasses."

The screen door slammed behind her and I listened to the gravel crackle and fade with her steps.

The front room wasn't much bigger than the kitchen, but Momma had managed to fill it with all sorts of furniture. Someday, Babe, we're gonna have a big house an' we're gonna need all this, she'd say. There were tables and chairs and a couch with a trundle bed under it. At night, when Momma didn't sleep with me, she'd have to put the coffee table in the kitchen so she could pull the bed out.

The front room had two big windows Momma had made heavy red curtains for. Light seeped in around them and through spaces in the clapboard walls, and dust settled on things in here like sand to the bottom of the creek.

I sprinkled water on the tee-shirt and sat down on the floor in front of the curio cabinet. Momma's curio cabinet had been a present from one of her men friend's years ago. It had sat empty in the corner of the front room 'til Gram died. Now its shelves were filled with Gram's china dogs.

Gram lived in the city. We hardly ever went there, but when we did, I always played with her dogs. Careful, she'd say. Them dogs come all the way from China an' oh were their paws sore when they got here. I believed her when I was real little. Really? I'd say and she'd smack her lips in a way that showed she was truly amazed herself.

We didn't go to the city when Gram died. Momma had company and couldn't get away. It was about a week later when a box arrived. Inside were Gram's dogs and a note from Momma's sister saying Gram wanted me to have them. Momma read the note then tossed it in the trash and walked outside. She didn't say anything when I put the dogs in the cabinet. Just looked at them, shook her head, then walked out again.

I snapped the glass door open and everybody inside clinked as they shuddered. On the top shelf was the big, red collie, his chest all puffed out. He was like a ballerina balancing on tiny, spindly legs. And when he walked, it was like he was prancing.

Two old white dogs with black spots made me think of Mutt and Jeff. They were street dogs, and the little chips in their ears were scars from dog fights they'd seen. Now they were just tough old friends, one always sleeping by the feet of the other.

The poodles were yippee little things, all frilly and delicate. Pretty to look at, but not much else. That's why they always stayed close to the bulldog. He took his place in front of them, feet turned in, muscles bulging out. Just to look at him was enough to stop you.

The momma dog on the bottom shelf had six little puppies. Three of them nursed while one slept between her front paws and the other two played in the grass next to her.

But my favorite was the mutt. He sat in one corner all shaggy and scraggly with one ear bent down. He was always watching out for everybody else. When it rained, he'd show the rest where they could get warm and dry. Then he'd go outside and curl up by himself in the cold. He took care of all of them and didn't need none of them to take care of him.

Their stories filled my head with all sorts of chatter as I brushed the dust off each of them and wiped their footprints from the glass shelves. Then I told them what good dogs they were, and I put them back where they belonged.

I saw the headlights like two little sparks bouncing down the road and hurried up with the dishes. I just had time to check the front room one more time, fluffing the pillows and smoothing the cover on the couch, when I heard the car door slam and Momma laughing.

The screen door squeaked open.

"Babe?"

I stood in the doorway to the front room, the tee-shirt behind my back.

"Babe, this here's Earl. He's a friend of mine." She looked back at the tall man with golden eyes, and he smiled from beneath his mustache. "This here's Chadaley Kathleen Ann Marie Gibbons, but I call her Babe. Go on in and make yourself at home. I'll be there in a minute."

I stepped back and Earl wedged himself by and into the front room.

"What'cha think, Babe? Nice, isn't he?" She was whispering.

"He's okay."

"You eat yet?" Momma pulled a pan out of the oven and a

can of tomato soup from the cupboard. "He's from California. Got himself his own mortuary there." She wedged the opener onto the can.

"He messes with dead people?"

"Well, somebody's got to do it. An' with the cost of funerals now-a-days, I bet he makes damn good money. An' anyhow, Babe, you've got to admit, he ain't never gonna be out of work. Not like a lot of men I know."

And Momma knew a lot of men. Momma dumped the soup into the pan and stirred in a can of water. She lit the burner then got down two glasses and pulled a bottle of whiskey out from under the sink.

"You can do this, can't ya, Babe? I got company." She grabbed my head and pulled it toward her before planting a kiss in the middle of my hair. "Thanks, Babe. "

I got the saltines out and stirred the soup 'til the lumps disappeared. Earl's voice was a low rumble from the front room and every now and then Momma's laugh would jump on top of it and I'd hear her say "Oh, Earl."

I always wondered how Momma kept them straight. Why she never said 'Oh, Sam' when it was Earl or 'Oh, Earl' when it was Sam, especially after one of them had stayed awhile. But she never did, I guess, 'cause I never heard one of them complain she didn't know who she was with.

That's what other people said. Momma had so many men she didn't know which one she was with the night before. But that wasn't true. Momma always knew. And she always remembered them.

"Remember Jake?" she'd say. "You know, the one with the scar through his eyebrow?" Or "I wonder whatever happened to Billy. He sure had the softest hands."

I crumbled the saltines over my soup. They were like snow over a red sea, and I watched as they slowly turned to a pink-tinged mush. Momma came rushing in.

"Ain't you done yet? I swear, Babe. Let me have some of them, would ya." She pulled a column of crackers from the box then rifled through the cupboard. "You didn't eat those sardines, did ya, Babe? You know I save those for company."

I stood on my chair and reached over her head to the top shelf.

"Thanks, Babe." She took the sardines out of my hand and grabbed a handful of napkins. "Now hurry up an' eat. You otta be gittin' to bed pretty soon, don'cha think?"

The saltines had melted in the soup, and I fished them out 'til I scraped the last one off the bottom of the bowl. I ran water in the bowl and pan, poured myself a glass of milk and stood in the doorway to the front room.

Momma had Earl all wrapped up, her hair and arms molded around his shoulders like hot wax. He sat there, his hands telling a story in front of him, probably about some dead person he found particularly interesting. Momma looked back at me. She winked and mouthed, "Night, Babe."

I shut the bedroom door and scrunched up on the bed next to the headboard. Momma's laughter creeped in anyway. I couldn't hear Earl anymore, but I knew he was still talking 'cause Momma was still laughing. Pretty soon, I heard the coffee table bump into the kitchen.

"Careful, Earl. You'll wake Babe."

I didn't have to hear Momma say it. I just knew she would. I turned off the light so Momma wouldn't see it and pulled the covers up, over my clothes and all.

I woke up to the crash and Momma's yelling, "Earl, stop it!"

There was more glass breaking and a thud.

The next sound was Momma too, but she wasn't saying anything, just kind of making a noise.

I kicked out from under the covers and jerked the door open. Things were still banging around, and I could see giant shadows dancing across the ceiling of the front room and into the kitchen.

Momma wasn't saying anything, and all I could hear from Earl was a lot of breathing, heavy and coarse. I climbed up on top of the coffee table and scrambled to the front room.

Earl was across the room in his underwear. He had Momma against the wall where the curio cabinet used to be. His hands were around her neck, and she was scratching and kicking at him.

The whiskey bottle was rolling around the middle of the trundle bed and I grabbed it up. I don't really remember hitting Earl with it, but when I did he let go. He turned around to me, but I still had what was left of the bottle in my hand, and I pointed it right at his face.

"Get out of here, Earl!" Momma remembered their names even when she shouldn't of been able to. She was pushing herself up against the wall. I just stood there, that bottle an inch away from Earl's face.

"Get out, or we'll both kill you!"

I guess the threat of getting killed twice was what it took, cause Earl grabbed up his clothes and climbed over the bed past me. The kitchen door banged into the coffee table when he tried to open it, and he whacked that thing into that table 'til it come plumb off its hinges and he could get out.

I looked at Momma. Her hair was all in her face and when she pushed it back I saw that her lip was bleeding, and she had a cut on her cheek. She leaned against the wall and looked at me.

"Well, Babe. I certainly wouldn't call that molasses. Why don't you let me have that thing?"

She put her hand out for the bottle, but I wasn't ready to let go just yet. She ended up having to pry my fingers one by one from around the neck of it. I helped her put the trundle bed back away, and we carried the coffee table in from the kitchen. Momma leaned the kitchen door in place, then she smoothed the cover on the couch and fluffed the pillows. She stood up and looked around the room, her eyes locking on the tipped over curio cabinet.

"Oh, Babe. Momma's dogs." She knelt down in the middle of the shattered glass and broken china and picked up the collie, his hind legs missing. "Oh, Momma. I'm sorry. I'm so sorry." She swept through the broken pieces 'til she found the missing legs then pieced them together puzzle-like. Mamma's shoulders began to shake.

"Momma?" I stood next to her, my hand on her shoulder. Momma was crying.

In all the Sam's and Jake's and Earl's that had come and gone, Momma never cried once. Not when Gram died or even when my real daddy left.

"Momma?" I patted her on the shoulder. "It's all right. I can fix him. I can fix them all, Momma."

Momma grabbed me around the waist and pulled me to her. I pushed back, but I couldn't hold her off. Her arms wrapped fast around me, and I let go, curling up inside of them. She buried her face in my hair, and I pushed myself as hard against her as I could. Her arms drew in tighter and her body shuddered with her tears. Then mine came too.

When I woke up the next morning, Momma and me was on the couch, and she had hot cocoa on the coffee table.

It took all day, but we pieced Gram's dogs back together. The poodles aren't quite as frilly, but the bulldog didn't even have a scratch. You can hardly see the line on the collie's legs and the others got put back together almost as good.

Only the mutt couldn't be fixed. Momma says she thinks Earl probably stepped on him. We found all the pieces we could and Momma got a little box to put them in. We keep it in the curio cabinet with the other dogs 'cause Momma says China's too far to come from just to get thrown away.

Anyway, she says, it's a good way of rememberin' Earl, and we don't ever want to forget him. As if Momma ever could.

1993

Double Jeopardy

It had been so easy. Just one blow with a ten-pound barbell.

He cleaned the chrome weight, wiped the spots of blood from the wall, washed and shaved, then changed his clothes. Now, he wrapped the body carefully, almost reverently, in a clean white sheet.

For twenty-three years he had waited for this day. For twenty-three years, he had planned and schemed and directed his every action toward this moment, toward his vindication.

Twenty-three years ago he had been a young, vibrant entrepreneur who stormed the corporate world and quickly established himself as no ordinary contender. All his dreams were within his reach. Then his wife of eight years had asked for a divorce and demanded half of everything he had acquired. He had refused and quickly moved assets and rearranged capital out of her grasp. That was when, he was sure, she had devised her plan.

In his mind, he could see her moving through the house one last time, checking every last detail as she went. She was so precise, such a perfectionist; moving a lamp slightly to the right, changing the position of a vase, arranging the shoe prints in the blood, her hair on the bookend. When she walked out the door for the last time, for her it meant a rebirth with a new identity. For him, it meant total destruction.

That January night, the police had responded to his frantic call to find the house ransacked, jewelry and money gone, and blood staining the living room carpet. Her body never was found, but the police contrived a motive and enough circumstantial evidence to convince a jury that he had faked the robbery and murdered his wife.

Now, he had murdered her.

He carried her body to the car and gently curled it into the trunk. He hesitated, then folded back the sheet from her face. Yes, he thought, her face must be visible when the trunk lid opens. It must be the first thing Burk sees.

When he first saw her, he was surprised at how different and yet how much the same she was. She smoked now, and wore her make-up heavy. She had let her hair go back to its natural brown and wore it in tight curls. And there was a grace to her movements he didn't remember. But there were also the habits so ingrained in us that we are not even aware of their existence.

There was the way she brushed her hair back behind her ear, with the back of her nails rather than her fingertips. And the way she leaned into a conversation, then fell back into her chair when her point was made. And her laughter. A little deeper than before maybe, but still the same trill that began deep inside and grew until it burst forth in a loud chortle.

For three months he studied her and, as he did, he became aware of his own idiosyncrasy that he would need to change. There was his habit of tapping his cigarette three times, then twice more before lighting it. He quit smoking.

And the way he tied his shoelaces, first in a bow and then by knotting the two loops together. He bought loafers.

And the habit he had of clearing his throat before speaking. That was the hardest one to alter. Once, after he had orchestrated their meeting and they had started seeing each other, he caught himself slipping back into the habit. She had looked at him curiously. A cold, he said. After that he carried mints and always tried to have one in his mouth when he was with her.

It would be a four-hour drive to Georgetown. He called the police station before leaving. He wanted to be sure Burk would be there. It couldn't be just anyone. Burk had been the main force behind the investigation. It had been quite a coup for him to topple such a successful businessman. From his prison cell, he had followed Burk's rise through the ranks; first sergeant, then lieutenant, and now captain. Yes, Burk had to be the one.

He followed her to Mexico, to a small resort town on the coast. He arranged for their first encounter to be on the tennis court, a bit of an irony as she had sworn his attempts at teaching her to play would be the death of her. He feigned ineptness. She lavished him with patience and good-humored advice. Their courtship was filled with sailing and dancing, laughter and lovemaking. Three months later, they married and for a month she shared his home just two hundred miles from where she had walked out on him twenty-three years earlier.

"It's Captain Burk now, isn't it.?" He had to speak loudly to be heard over the din of the squad room.

"Yeah, it is. What can I do you for." Burk turned to face him, and he let the detective study him, search his face for some clue to his identity.

"I'm Charles Greyson. Remember me?"

"Greyson?!"

He smiled at the surprise in the Captain's voice.

"Why are *you* here?"

"Twenty-three years ago you arrested me for the murder of my wife."

"Yeah. And nine months later you were convicted."

Still condescending, he thought. It would add pleasure to his vindication.

"I was innocent."

"The jury didn't think so."

He smiled. "If I might have a moment of your time. I have something to show you in my car. It won't take long."

He turned to lead the way, but stopped when Burk did not follow.

"You need not be concerned. It is not reprisal I am after. As I told you twenty-three years ago, I am not a violent man."

"What are you doing here, Greyson?"

"I will show you. This way . . . please."

He led the way down the hall and Burk followed.

"This is about your wife, isn't it?"

"Of course it is."

"So what is it you want? Did somebody call you?"

They had reached the rear of Greyson's car.

"I spent twenty years in prison for the murder of my wife, even though you couldn't even produce a body. Well, Captain, I found her."

"You *what*?"

"It took almost every penny I had left and two years of searching, but I found her. Now that's something not even this state's best detective can claim, is it, Captain?"

"Greyson, I think you better stop right there . . . "

He turned the key in the lock and the trunk sprang open.

"Captain, may I present to you . . . my wife."

She lay just as he had placed her, gently wrapped in white, a thin stream of blood just visible beneath her curls. His breath came heavy with exhilaration. He could feel his heart pounding his satisfaction. He turned to relish the expression in Burk's eyes.

The Captain stared at the woman in the trunk, his face creased, his eyes squinting. He swallowed hard and had to wet his lips before he could speak.

"Mr. Greyson, I don't know who this is in this trunk, but we just identified a body found west of town and your wife is in our morgue."

1991

For Children

Angel on my Shoulder

Vanessa's mother? She just loves me. She's always tryin' to get me to go to church with them, but I don't get up Sunday mornings. If I want church, I just watch channel twenty-one. That's all. That's enough for me.

Oooo. My reading teacher? Now that is one ugly lady. She reminds me of you. Always getting up in my face and all. Told me the very first day she didn't like me. She's got me sitting right up front. I hate that. Close enough to smell the olive oil on her breath. I bought some Tic-Tacs. Gave her the whole box.

But she's nasty. Always sayin' stuff. There was this assembly? And these dancers did the splits? And she was all sayin', 'I can do that.' Like I wanted to know. Turned my stomach up just to think about it. She shouldn't be doin' that. Tellin' us about her private life and all. That's nasty.

There was a condom in the room! Right on the floor! She told me I was disturbing her class an' did I want to go to the office. I told her that condom was more disturbing than me. They was all throwing pencils at it, pokin' it and stuff. She's always askin' if I want to go to the office. I told her, "Sure, let's go," and she didn't do nothin'. I saw my counselor and

131

he says I'm givin' that teacher a hard time an' I gotta cool my attitude.

Mrs. Cormski, she's the counselor at North? That's where I'm goin' next year. She's lookin' out for me. Got all the security guards at Hill checkin' me out. They're always askin', "You still doin' okay for Mrs. Cromski?" I tell 'em, "Yeah." Almost got in a fight, though. Some girl was out for me. Don't know why. She got all up in my face but I told her, "You better get them clothes back to Goodwill," and she didn't do nothin'.

I'm in ROTC. Rangers and drill team. My back is sore! We gotta run up them bleachers with weights. We ran up those bleachers an' then them other ones! Had to do it three times. Then run the track twice and sprint once. Me? I just took my time. Stopped to tie my shoe, fix the strap on the weights. Thirty pounds of sand. Oooo, my back is sore. I think I got a bruise. I still beat them though. They were all ahead, but then the last two times around the track? I kicked ass an' passed them all.

Drill team? We got wooden rifles. We twirl them around and stuff. Monique, she's on rifle team. Oooo, she's good! Bam, bam, bam! She hits them all right in the middle. I got to decide if I want to stick with drill team or do Rangers. You know, it's like, camping, twirling. Twirling, camping. I think I'll go camping.

I'm getting A's. A "B" in science, but he hardly teaches us anything. Tells us to read page twenty-eight to seventy-four and do the questions at the end. I can't hardly stand it. I'm in honors English. I still got all them papers Mrs. Bradley gave us on conflict and paragraphs and stuff. She asks me a question an' I just look it up. Irony and resolution, I think. I got to do a Socratic presentation. I got to find me something good to read. Them other kids all read poems and the class just sat there. She gave 'em lousy grades. I thought up questions like, what do you think of a story like that. But I got to find me something good to read.

When I get to North? I'm gonna do sports. Track an' basketball. Mrs. Cromski? She says that's my ticket, that's how I'll get to college. Mrs. Cormski, she's lookin' out for me.

The Tear of a Dragon

She told me it was the tear of a dragon, and I never doubted her. It hung about her neck on a chain far too heavy for an object so delicate, and whenever I pleased her, she would let me hold it.

"Careful," she would say. "If you drop it, it will break into a million teardrops from a million dragons."

I could not imagine one dragon, let alone a million, small enough to shed tears so tiny. Yet still, because she had said so, I would caress the crystalline object in my hands, the chain wrapped a half dozen times around my fingers, just in case.

And when she wasn't looking I would grasp the chain tightly and let the object dangle in front of me. Transfixed, I would sit, watching light dance through the object in a multitude of colors.

She stood at the kitchen counter, her back to me, molding the dough before her. I held the object before me and stared into its center.

"Grandma, tell me how you got it."

"I've told you that before." The rolling pin squeaked

rhythmically as she pressed the dough into its perfect circle.

"I know. But I want to hear it again. About the wizard and all."

She took the cookie cutters from the shelf and pulled the step up to the counter.

"Well," she started, "It all happened many years ago when I was about the size you are now."

She took the chain from me and with flour-dusted hands hooked it back around her neck. I listened intently as she unrolled the tale as she had so many times before. I could not remember back far enough to the first time I had heard the story and never thought to question how she could always be the size I was "now".

I cut the cookies, and she slipped the out-of-season Santa Clauses and reindeers onto the baking sheet, only they had become wizards and unicorns. My mind hung on every word she spoke as if I had never before heard such sounds. And though I could quote much of the story by heart, I never thought to do so. It was my grandmother's story and some unspoken, unchallengeable creed declared that she alone could tell it. No one else could have made the brambles as sharp or the wizard as tall as my grandmother.

I watched as she slipped the last sheet of cookies into the oven. She stood up and looked at me.

"And that's how I came to have it, the tear of the dragon."

I took two still warm cookies from the cooling rack.

"And I didn't even know dragons could cry," I said.

"Neither did I." She poured two glasses of milk and sat down beside me.

I watched the object sparkle as she moved. "And if I

dropped it?" I asked.

"It would shatter into a million tears from a million dragons." Her hands flew up as if scattering a million tiny objects, and I jerked back to make room for such a multitude in such a small kitchen.

It wasn't long after that, that my mother was transferred by her employer, and we moved away from my grandmother. We went back frequently to visit, but never again were there times when my grandmother and I could sit alone and just talk.

I was nineteen when she died, and we went back one last time. My mother, with her sisters and brothers and their daughters and sons, met at the house, and I watched as they cleaned out the closets and divided up the memories. Pictures and books, letters and curios were carefully discussed and assigned new ownership.

My mother handed me the box. Its lid was tied shut, and my name was scribbled across the top. I stepped out onto the back porch. The string fell from the box, and I lifted the lid. I took the object from its cotton bed and slipped it into my pocket.

The long shadows of trees split the road as I walked toward the woods. I felt the object in my pocket and found myself unconsciously wrapping its chain a half dozen times around my fingers. Its multitude of sides and edges were smooth, familiar to my touch.

The sun barely shown above the ridge by the time I reached the clearing. At the center, I clambered to the top of the large rock and looked at the dark woods surrounding me. I thought of all that the shadows hid from view even in the daylight and knew that unicorns and wizards were among them.

I took the object from my pocket and carefully unwrapped the chain from my fingers. The sun's last rays glimmered through it as it dangled before me. My fist closed tight around it, and I raised it high above my head. I hesitated, standing there, hand in air, as if giving one final salute. Then I closed my eyes, held my breath and waited for a million dragons to cry.

Plays

An Interruption

A one-act play

olivia's first play, An Interruption, was selected as the first place winner in a competition sponsored by Arizona State University Women and the American Association of University Women and produced in Tempe in 1982.

LIST OF CHARACTERS

Sally Kinsey .... A young housewife who would like
                         to be a writer
Will Kinsey............... Sally's business-minded husband
Addie .... The main character in Sally's story
Ginny .... Addie's older sister
Robert .... Addie's oldest son

SCENE ONE

Scene: The setting is the studio
apartment of SALLY and WILL
KINSEY. It is a small apartment,
sparsely furnished in "early American
poverty." Off center on the back wall
is a small fireplace. A filled woodbox
sits next to it. To one side of the stage
is a double bed made somewhat to
look like a couch with a table and

141

lamp next to it. A door near the bed leads to the unseen bathroom. On the other side of the stage is the kitchen. A small window over the sink looks out on a dreary world. A table with two chairs sits nearby. A door leads from the kitchen to the hall outside. There is very little other furniture, except for a rocking chair and perhaps an overstuffed chair near the fireplace.

The curtains along the wings and the back of the stage suggest the walls of the apartment. The entrances and exits of SALLY and WILL are determined by the reality of their apartment, but the characters of Sally's story are not so limited. Their movements are frequently through the "walls" of the Kinsey apartment.

For SALLY and WILL the time is fall in the early 1960s. For the characters in SALLY's story, it is the same season in the mid-1930s, the time of the Great Depression.

At rise: It is late afternoon, about four o'clock, and the first chill of the season settles in the room despite a low burning fire. Empty pans and unused utensils on the kitchen counter suggest that someone has begun dinner but not gotten very far.

The stage is dark except for a light that spots Sally as she sits writing at the kitchen table. She is a woman in her late twenties, a young housewife anxious to please her husband yet trying to be herself. She is dressed casually in slacks and jacket to ward

off the autumn chill. As she scribbles
into a well-used spiral notebook, we
hear her voice telling us what it is she
is writing.

SALLY'S VOICE

The fire had been dying for some time now.
(Lights come up slowly revealing
Addie, a woman who could not be
older than thirty two, yet whose
appearance suggests one of much
greater age. She is simply dressed in
the style of the 1930s, almost dowdy
in appearance. A shawl hangs loosely
from her shoulders. She sits in the
rocking chair staring at the fireplace.)
Addie sat in front of it, transfixed by the ever-changing shapes
of the glowing embers. The shawl had slipped from her
shoulders, yet she seemed unaware of the chill in the room. It
was Robert's voice that brought her back to cold reality.

(ROBERT enters dressed in rumpled
bedclothes. He is fourteen years old,
but with the mannerisms of a man.
SALLY continues to write as he and
ADDIE converse.)

ROBERT

Mother?

(ADDIE looks up. ROBERT notices the
dying fire and speaks to ADDIE as if
reprimanding a child.)
You've let the fire die down. The house will be cold when
father gets home.

(He crosses to the fireplace.)

ADDIE
(Pulling the shawl up on to her
shoulders, she speaks with quiet,
almost sad resignation.)
I guess I fell asleep. You go back to bed, Robert. I'll tend to the

fire.

>   (ADDIE makes no move toward the
>   woodbox and ROBERT continues
>   to speak to her in a condescending,
>   parental manner.)

ROBERT

I can get it as long as I'm here.

>   (He takes wood from the box and puts
>   it on the fire.)

Is father still in town?

ADDIE

It's Saturday. I suppose he has stopped at the tavern.

ROBERT

He has a right to, you know.

ADDIE

I suppose he does.

ROBERT

He works hard. It's not like he doesn't take care of us. We eat
well enough. And we haven't lost our home like some people
have.

ADDIE

You're right about that. Thomas does provide for us.

>   (ROBERT starts to get more wood
>   from the box, but stops short. He pulls
>   a razor strop out instead and turns
>   to ADDIE. She continue to watch the
>   dying fire, unaware of what he is
>   doing. Holding the strop up, ROBERT
>   snaps it making a loud sound. ADDIE
>   jumps, frightened by the sound. She
>   looks fearfully at the strop.)

ROBERT

What's this doing in here?

ADDIE
(She turns to the fire, pulling the shawl
tighter around her. Her monotone
answer conflicts with the fear she has
just shown.)
It fell. I was going to put it back in the morning ... before your
father missed it.

ROBERT
You don't think he'll miss it tonight?

ADDIE
Go to bed, Robert. Please. Before your father gets home.

ROBERT
All right.
(He hangs the strop on the wall above
the woodbox.)
I'll see you in the morning then. Goodnight, Mother.

(ROBERT exits at the same place from
which he entered. He doesn't hear
ADDIE's final words.)

ADDIE
I was only hoping he wouldn't miss it tonight.

WILL
(Off stage. Excited)
Sally? Sal!

(ADDIE looks fearfully towards his
voice. SALLY quickly finishes the
sentence she is writing and covers the
notebook with a dishtowel, obviously
to hide it. WILL enters. He is an
eager man, not quite thirty years old,
dressed in casual business attire. As he
comes through the door, ADDIE rises
suddenly, fearfully.)
Sally, guess what?

SALLY
(SALLY rises to greet Will lovingly).
Will, it's only 4:30. What are you doing home?
(SALLY hugs WILL as ADDIE
backs away from the scene and slowly
exits.)

WILL

Guess what.

SALLY

I don't know. What?

WILL

You know the project I was working on last week?

SALLY
The one for the new hydro system?
(WILL nods enthusiastically.)
They liked it?

WILL

Liked it? They loved it! Fitzpatrick called from Seattle. He said it was some of the best work he has seen in months. Sal, they're talking promotion. Promotion! Do you know what that means?
(Indicates the apartment.)
No more living in one-room apartments. No more Saturday nights at home. No more vacations at the park down the street. We could travel. Really travel!
(He looks directly at SALLY.)
And we could start a family, Sal.
(He sits down at the kitchen table.)
We could have kids. I could have a son! Just think of it. William Daniel Kinsey the Third.

SALLY
(Draping her arm affectionately
around WILL.)
You know something, William Daniel Kinsey the Second?

                              WILL
No. What?

                              SALLY
I love you and I'm very proud of you.
                              (She leans down and kisses him on the
                              cheek.)
And I'm going to fix you something special for all your hard
work .
                              (SALLY goes to the counter and opens
                              a cupboard.)
I was just about to start dinner.

                              WILL
Don't bother, hon. Not for me anyway. I'm meeting some of
the guys down at Fridays for a little celebration.
                              (SALLY's face registers
                              disappointment as she skips over
                              some food and pulls a can of soup
                              from the shelf.)
You know, I would have thought they'd be jealous. But not
Rick and the guys. Know what he said to me?

                              SALLY
No. What?

                              WILL
He said that he was glad it was me. That I deserve it. What do
you think of that?

                              SALLY
I think it's great. Will you be out late?

                              WILL
I don't know. Maybe. Hand me a beer, will you, Sal?
                              (With obvious disappointment that
                              WILL fails to notice, SALLY gets a
                              beer from the refrigerator.)
So how was your day?

SALLY

The usual.

> (She sets the beer on the table and
> returns to her can of soup.)

I finally got around to washing the window, though there's nothing out there worth seeing. It does look better, I suppose. What do you think?

WILL

You know, I'm glad I included that part about the impact of variable filters. They didn't ask for it, but I think it really impressed them that I put it in anyway. What did you say, hon?

SALLY

I said I washed the window finally. Do you think it looks better?

> (WILL turns to look at the window.)

WILL

Looks great.

> (As he turns back around to the table,
> he knocks over his beer.)

Damn!

> (He quickly picks up the can and
> grabs the towel covering the notebook
> and begins mopping up the spill. Sally
> grabs another towel and hurries to the
> table.)

SALLY

Here, I'll get it.

> (She finishes the job for WILL and
> takes the towels to the sink.)

WILL

I'm sorry, Sal. Anyway, the window does look great.

SALLY

Thank you.

                    WILL
                (Picking up the notebook.)
What's this?

                    SALLY
Nothing, really.

                (She takes the notebook from him,
                tosses it onto the counter and goes
                back to her dinner, her back to WILL.)

                    WILL
You're not still trying to write, are you?

                    SALLY
A little, I guess.

                (WILL goes to SALLY. He wraps
                his arms around her and holds her
                lovingly as he inconsiderately teases
                her.)

                    WILL
What about this time? Boogiemen under the stairs?
                (WILL nuzzles SALLY's neck, kissing
                it.)

                    SALLY
It's just a story.

                    WILL
Just a story, huh?   What about?
                (WILL continues to kiss the back of
                SALLY's neck, but she only minimally
                responds to his affection.)

                    SALLY
                (She shrugs off Will's feigned interest.)
A woman.

                    WILL
No one in particular?

SALLY

I guess not.

WILL

Well, I'll tell you what, Mrs. William Kinsey. When I get this promotion, you won't have time to worry about writing about no one in particular. And in the mean time...

> (He turns SALLY around to face him
> and passionately studies her face.)

... I 'm going to shower and get ready to go out, but when I get back ... I'll give you something worth writing about. (He kisses her.) Love you, babe.

> (WILL exits through the bathroom
> door. SALLY watches him leave then
> turns back to her dinner of soup.)

The Lights Come Down

SCENE TWO

Scene: It is late the same evening, almost 11 o'clock. The kitchen has been cleaned up but the rest of the apartment is much the same. A low fire continues to burn in the fireplace.

At rise: Dressed in a nightgown, SALLY sits in bed writing in her notebook by the light of the table lamp. The rest of the stage is dark. SALLY's voice-over of her writing begins the scene.

SALLY'S VOICE

Dear God, please. The words kept going through Addie's mind.

(The lights come up slowly and we see ADDIE sitting in a kitchen chair. Her blouse is unbuttoned, and she has allowed it to drop off her shoulders and back. GINNY is six years older than ADDIE but it's difficult to tell. She still has the appreciation and love for life that ADDIE lost so long ago.)

The pain lashed across her back as it had the night before. Her sister's hand was gentle and Addie knew that soon the salve would deaden the pain, but just now all she wanted was for Ginny to finish. So closed was she against her agony that she barely heard Ginny speak.

GINNY

He's going to kill you.

(She finishes with the salve and helps ADDIE pull her blouse onto her shoulders.)

Did you hear me Addie? That man is going to kill you. These beatings are getting worse.

ADDIE
(She answers without emotion as she
buttons her blouse.)

I know.

GINNY
(ADDIE's resignation to her situation
exasperates her.)

Then do something.

ADDIE

What am I do to, Gin?

GINNY

You know what I think you should do.

ADDIE

I can't. I've told you that.

GINNY
(She gestures angrily towards the
razor strop.)

Then the least you can do is get rid of that thing.

ADDIE
(Almost with indifference.)

I tried, but Robert found it and put it back.

GINNY
(To herself.)

Even your children.
(To ADDIE)

Addie, come away with us.
(ADDIE shakes her head.)

You know Joe and I both want you to. You could start a new
life out west... away from Thomas.

ADDIE

I can't.

GINNY

He doesn't even know we're planning on leaving.

ADDIE

Ginny, please.

GINNY

He wouldn't even know where to look for you.

ADDIE

Ginny …

GINNY

He'd never be able to find you.

ADDIE
(Disturbed with GINNY's persistence.)

… I can't.

GINNY

We'll leave in two weeks. We'll be gone before he knows it. He wouldn't even …

ADDIE
(She interrupts angrily.)

I wouldn't know what to do, how to live …

GINNY

Joe and I would help you.

ADDIE
(She confronts GINNY angrily.)

I can't just walk out on him. Not with the boys. Don't you understand! They love their father. They would never leave him. What do you want me to do, Ginny? Walk out on them, too?

GINNY
(Quietly, hesitantly.)

Yes.

                    ADDIE
            (ADDIE stares at GINNY. She can't
            believe what she has just heard.)
You can't mean that.

                    GINNY
If that's the only way ... yes... I do.
            (ADDIE turns away from GINNY.
            The thought of leaving her children is
            almost too much to consider; that her
            sister should suggest it is too much.
            Tears fill her eyes.)

                    GINNY
            (Continuing.)
Addie ... has he ever beat either of the boys?

                    ADDIE
Thomas? He's hardly ever spanked them, but ...

                    GINNY
Then they'll be all right.

                    ADDIE
But they're my boys, Ginny.
            (She turns to face GINNY.)
They're my children. How could you even suggest such a
thing? I could never leave them. They're my babies.

                    GINNY
They are their father's sons.
            (ADDIE stares at her sister. She
            is still confused, taken aback by
            GINNY's suggestion. And now the
            implication of GINNY's words terrifies
            her. ADDIE searches for her own
            explanation.)

                        154

ADDIE

You're jealous, aren't you? That's what it is. You want me to leave my children because you can't have any and you're jealous.

GINNY

Addie, you know that's not true.

ADDIE

Yes, it is. You've always been jealous of my boys.

GINNY

No, Addie! Envious, yes. Hurt because I would never have children of my own, yes. But I have never wanted anything but the best for you and you know it.

ADDIE
(Angrily.)
Then why?

GINNY

Because I want you to live… Why do you think Robert hung the strop back on the wall?

ADDIE
(She staunchly defends her son.)
He wanted his father to be able to find it this morning.

GINNY

Don't you think he knew what his father was going to do with it last night? He's fourteen years old, Addie. How long is it going to be before he makes use of that strop himself?

ADDIE

But what about Dan? He's only nine. He's different. He's not like Robert.

GINNY

He's only nine this year. Addie, they will grow into the men they've been taught to become.

ADDIE

Well, maybe I can change that. Maybe I can make a difference. At least with Dan.

GINNY

If you can teach him to question his father. If he ignores what he sees. If he doesn't take after his brother, and if you live long enough.

ADDIE
(ADDIE begins to break down and the tears begin to flow.)
But they're my babies, Ginny. They're my babies.
(ADDIE breaks into long, heavy sobs and turns away from GINNY.)
They're my babies.

GINNY
(GINNY wraps her arms around ADDIE as if comforting a hurt child.)
Oh, Addie. My poor Addie. I don't want you to hurt. Please understand. I'm just so frightened for you, so scared I'm going to move away and never see you again. I don't want to lose you, Addie. I don't want to lose you.
(GINNY holds her sister close to her, gently rocking and stroking her hair. ADDIE's sobs subside into quiet tears.)
Addie, do you remember when Papa died?

ADDIE
(Shakes her head.)
I was only four.

GINNY

I remember. It was just before harvest. Mama held you on her hip and me by the hand as she brought us home from the cemetery. She took us home alone. Wouldn't let anyone come with us. Neighbors had brought all sorts of food over and the house smelled like Thanksgiving and Christmas together. Mama put you down an told me to go get Papa's walking stick. Do you remember Papa's walking stick?

          (ADDIE shakes her head.)

It was a hickory cane. I can remember the sound it made when he hit it across the tabletop. Mama took it from me and threw it into the fire. Then she held us close to her and cried the rest of the night. Addie.

          (She lifts ADDIE's face to look at her.)

When that horse threw Papa, it saved Mama's life. I don't think she would have left Papa. I know she would never have left us. But I also know, Addie … I also know I used to pray that she would.

          (GINNY pulls ADDIE close to her and
          ADDIE holds tight.)

Think about what I said. Please. Promise me you'll think about coming with us.

          (There is the sound of keys dropping
          outside the door of the apartment.
          SALLY looks up from her writing. All
          stage lights except for the lamp next to
          SALLY begin to come down. GINNY
          continues to hold ADDIE, gently
          rocking her.

          SALLY slips the notebook and pen
          under the bed and turns the lamp out
          leaving the stage in dark shadows.
          SALLY lies down and feigns sleep as
          WILL enters, obviously drunk. He
          closes the door and clumsily makes his
          way across the apartment. He kneels
          beside the bed and awkwardly strokes
          SALLY's hair. SALLY doesn't move.)

WILL
(Quietly and slurred.)
Sally? You asleep? Hey, baby. Your man's home.

The Lights Come Down

SCENE THREE

Scene: It is early morning a few days later. The apartment has the rushed look of getting up and off to work. The table is set for breakfast and a newspaper lies on top of SALLY's notebook between the place settings. A dish towel haphazardly covers an old, black lunch pail on the counter. It is inconspicuous to the audience. The fire in the fireplace barely burns.

At rise: SALLY, dressed in a housecoat, hurries about the kitchen getting breakfast for WILL. As she puts his coffee on the table, WILL enters from the bathroom. He is wearing his best suit and is groomed to a tee.

                    WILL
Well, how do I look?

                    SALLY
Beautiful, even if I do say so myself.
                    (She kisses him good morning then
                    goes back to getting breakfast ready.)
I'll have French toast here shortly.

                    WILL
Oh, Sally. I'm sorry. I'm too excited to eat a thing. I'm just glad Fitzpatrick wants to see me this morning. If I had to wait 'till this afternoon …

                    SALLY
                    (Finishing for him.)
You would still do great. Now sit down and drink your coffee. I have to get something.
                    (SALLY crosses to the bed.)

159

                    WILL
What are you up to now?

                    SALLY
                    (She stoops down to retrieve
                    something from under the bed.)
Nothing, you just read your paper.
                    (As SALLY searches under the bed,
                    WILL picks up the paper and sits
                    down at the kitchen table. Noticing
                    the notebook, he puts the paper down
                    and picks it up instead. He glances
                    through it and stops at a random
                    page.)

                    WILL
                    (He reads from the notebook as if
                    mimicking a soap opera.)
Addie stood in the doorway watching until the top of Dan's
head disappeared below the hill. Her jaw still hurt. He said he
was sorry. He hadn't meant for the cup to hit her.
                    (To SALLY)
Sal, are you serious about this?
                    (WILL turns to the next page in the
                    notebook. SALLY slowly stands, a
                    shirt box with a big bow on it in her
                    hands. As WILL begins to read again,
                    she pulls the box close to her body,
                    as if to protect herself from WILL's
                    stinging words.)

                    WILL
                    (He continues to read in the same
                    mimicking tone.)
She sat in the dark trying to write a letter to Dan, to explain,
to apologize, to reassure him. But each time it seemed useless.
What could she say that her leaving would not contradict?
She could not save him if she left. She could not save herself
if she stayed.
                    (WILL looks at SALLY and sees the
                    box.)

What you got there?

SALLY
(Trying to disguise her hurt as she
gives the box to WILL.)
Just a little congratulations present.

WILL
I don't have the promotion, yet.

SALLY
You will before the day's out. Go ahead. Open it.
(WILL opens the box and takes out a
white dress shirt.)
If you're going to move up in this world, you're going to need
a decent shirt.

WILL
Sal, that's nice.

SALLY
Look.
(She grabs the cuff and shows it to
WILL.)
I even had it monogrammed. W.D.K. It's not much, but maybe
next promotion I can get you a new suit.

WILL
It's wonderful, Sal. And so are you.
(He stands and kisses her.)
But if I'm going to move up in this world, I'd better not be late.
I'll call you around noon to tell you how things go.
(WILL hurries out the door.)

SALLY
(Calling after him.)

Good luck.

(SALLY begins to clean up the kitchen.
The hurt she hid before begins to
show and her movements are slow,
methodical and sad. She clears the
table and slips WILL's new shirt back
into the box. Picking up the notebook,
she brushes it off with the corner of
her housecoat. The lights come down.
SALLY sets the notebook down and
slips her housecoat off. Beneath it, she
is dressed in slacks and a blouse. As
she sits down a light spots her. The
fire in the fireplace begins to burn
brighter. It is several hours later.

SCENE FOUR

> (As SALLY begins to write, we again
> hear her voice describing her words.)

SALLY's VOICE

He was gone ... finally. The morning had been hectic. Addie
had burned the breakfast and it made Thomas late and angry.
She was so afraid he would notice she was nervous or the
boys would ask her what was wrong.

> (Lights come up on stage and ADDIE
> enters dressed almost as before, but
> with an apron.)

Now she had only to wait for Robert to leave and for Ginny
and Joe to come by for her.

ROBERT
> (Entering.)

Mother?

> (ADDIE turns toward him, startled.
> ROBERT speaks to her harshly.)

Is that all you wanted from town? Just some lard and flour?

ADDIE

That's all.

ROBERT

I don't see why you can't wait and get this with the rest of
your shopping.

ADDIE

Please, Robert. Just go and get it for me.

ROBERT

All right. But if you ask me, I think it's a wasted trip.

> (ROBERT starts to exit, but noticing
> Thomas's lunch pail under the
> dishtowel on the counter he uncovers
> it. He turns to ADDIE scolding.)

You didn't give father his lunch.

ADDIE
(Picking up the pail, she holds it out to
him.)
If you hurry, you should be able to catch him.

ROBERT
(Shaking his head.)
I've got to get to town, remember. If he doesn't come back for
it, I'll take it to him later. Anyway, he's probably on his way
back for it now.

(ROBERT exits. ADDIE hesitates then
quickly puts the lunch pail down
and takes her apron off. She pulls an
obviously heavy suitcase from behind
the curtain. Throwing a shawl around
her shoulders, she hurries to the
window and anxiously looks out. She
turns back to the lunch pail and stares
at it.)

ADDIE
(To herself.)
Dear God, Ginny. Please hurry.

(The door of the apartment flies open
and ADDIE swings around to face it.)
Ginny?

(WILL enters and SALLY jumps up
startled. ADDIE freezes.)

WILL
Mrs. William Kinsey, welcome to prosperity. You are now
the wife of the regional supervisor for Hydro-Systems
International, and I'm taking you out to lunch to celebrate.

SALLY
Will, that's wonderful.

(She turns back to the notebook.)
Just let me finish …

                         WILL
                    (Interrupting.)
No ifs, ands, or buts, young lady.
                    (He picks up the notebook.)

                         SALLY
                    (Mildly protesting.)
Will.

                         WILL
                    (Continuing.)
Life is passing us by ...
                    (He tips the notebook as if it were a
                    hat.)
. . .and we are not going to miss any more of it.
                    (WILL tosses the notebook into the
                    fireplace.)

                         SALLY
Will, no!

                         WILL
                    (He continues talking, totally oblivious
                    to SALLY's protest.)
So get yourself ready, Mrs. Kinsey, and I'll ...
                    (He kisses SALLY.)
... spruce myself up a little.
                    (WILL exits into the bathroom. SALLY
                    stares after him. WILL's action have
                    caught her off guard, confused her.
                    She turns to the fireplace and realizes
                    the notebook is burning.)

SALLY

Oh, God, Addie!

> (Hurrying to the fireplace, she makes a desperate attempt to retrieve the notebook. ADDIE turns and stares past SALLY and into the fire. ADDIE begins to back slowly away as SALLY continues to try and retrieve the notebook.)

No!...Damn it! ... Ow! ... Damn it! ... Addie!... No!... I can't get it.

> (Realizing her efforts are futile, SALLY pulls back from the fire.)

I can't get it, Addie.

> (ADDIE reaches the edge of the set and exits, backing off.)

I can't get it ... Oh, Addie. Oh, God I'm sorry.

> (SALLY turns to look at ADDIE. Realizing she is gone, she stops short. She slowly stands continuing to stare at the place where ADDIE had stood. SALLY calls her name quietly.)

Addie?

> (SALLY glances around as if trying to find her, then turns quickly back to the fireplace. Slowly ADDIE's reality seeps into SALLY's consciousness. She turns to stare at the bathroom door where WILL exited. She cries out, almost screaming her anguish.)

Will!

WILL
(Off stage.)

Love you, babe.

The Curtain Falls.

Common Ground

Cast of Characters

Sandy Hall.................. woman in her mid-thirties, athletic

Mrs. Patton.................. woman in her late sixties, smartly
dressed, properly mannered

Scene: The setting is the main floor of
the home of SANDY HALL and the
recently deceased Karen Patton. It is
a large old house. The kitchen is off
stage right. A swinging door separates
it from the living-dining room that
takes up most of the stage. The front
door and entry are to the rear of stage
left and a stair leading to the second
floor is near the center of the back of
the stage. A door under the stair leads
to the basement.

The house has the appearance of
being well lived in. Furnishings were
obviously chosen for their comfort
rather than style. An old desk sits
near the kitchen door next to a full
and somewhat disheveled bookcase.
A phone sits on the desk. Near the
center of the living room a couch,
over-stuffed chair and rocker encircle
a coffee table in front of a fireplace

at stage left. To one side is a stereo.
An old wood table with mismatched
chairs occupies the dining area.
Keepsakes that take up corners and
photos and posters on walls indicate
the women of the house were lovers
with a respect for their womanhood
and Lesbianism. A framed photo
of the two women in a raft holds
prominence on the desk.

Yet there is a vacant feeling about
the house: a sense that the lives that
have been living here have been
unexpectedly interrupted. Several
days worth of mail lays scattered on
the floor below the mail drop in the
wall next to the front door. One glove
lays near by next to an empty coat
rack. Two unused place settings are
neatly arranged on the dining room
table and in the center of the table a
dead rose sits in a vase. A crystal wine
glass is in front of one place setting.
Its mate lays on its side on the coffee
table, its contents long evaporated.
Near it is an empty wine bottle.
Seemingly out of place on the set are
two stacks of boxes at the foot of the
stairs. They have no relationship to the
rest of the room.

At rise: It is mid-morning on a
Sunday in February. A winter storm
has surrounded the house with new
snow and filled it with a heavy chill. A
light snow continues to fall. As lights
come up on stage, MRS. PATTON
descends the stair. She is a woman in
her late sixties, smartly dressed and
very precise in her movements. She is
out of place in this well lived-in house

and her attire is slightly too dressy for
the household task at hand. She goes
directly to the boxes and carries one
stack of them upstairs.

As MRS. PATTON exits through a
bedroom door, SANDY HALL enters
through the front door. She is in her
mid-thirties, warmly dressed in boots,
hat, muffler, a heavy coat and one
glove. Her movements tell us she
is familiar with this old house. She
quickly closes the door behind her,
stamping the snow from her boots.

SANDY
(Picking up glove)
Hell of a lot of good you're doing me down there.
(Begins to remove her snow attire,
hanging it on the coat rack; calls)
Mr. C? Mr. ...
(Feeling the vacant atmosphere of the
rest of the house for the first time she
stops short. Her next words are with
quiet resignation, almost fear.)
Damn it, Karen.
(Quickly, she finishes with her hat and
coat, gathers the mail and calls again.)
Mr. C.
(To herself; shivering)
Shit it's cold in here.
(Drops mail on desk and checks
thermostat on wall)
Mr. C. Kitty, kitty, kitty.
(Picks up phone and dials; calling
again.)
I'm home. Come out, come out whereever you are ...
(Aside)
... if you haven't frozen your butt off.
(Into phone)
Kelly? This is Sandy Hall. I'm back home so you won't have

to worry about feeding the cat.
                    (Pause; taps and jiggles thermostat.)
As well as can be expected, I suppose.
                    (Quickly changing subject.)
Hey, do you know what happened to the heat in here? It's
cold as ice.
                    (Pause)
That's par for Keiser Power. I'll probably have to re-light the
pilot. Thanks for taking care of Mr. C. Ah …
                    (Hesit
                    ates)
I've decided to give the house up. I want to be out of here by
the end of the month so if you know anyone that's looking
…
                    (Pause)
Sure, I'll let you know if I do. Thanks again.
                    (Hangs up receiver and rummages
                    through desk drawer; not finding
                    what she is looking for there, she goes
                    to next drawer; slams drawer shut.)
All right, Karen. Where the hell did you hide the flashlight?
                    (SANDY exits through kitchen door
                    as MRS. PATTON enters at the top of
                    the stairs, carrying a box filled with
                    clothes, and begins to descend.)

                    SANDY
                    (Entering from kitchen)
In the tool drawer, where else? We'll have heat in a minute
Mr.…
                    (Stops short as she almost runs into
                    MRS. PATTON.)
… Lord give me shit. Mrs. Patton!

                    MRS. PATTON
                    (Sets box down and responds coolly,
                    properly)
Sandy.

                    SANDY
What are you doing here?

MRS. PATTON
(Straightening garments at the top of box)
I let myself in. I hope you don't mind. I've come to collect Karen's things.

SANDY
(Still startled by MRS. PATTON'S appearance; what has been said has not yet registered.)
But how did you get in? Did Kelly let you in? If that little twirp let you in and didn't tell me ...

MRS. PATTON
No one let me in. I have Karen's key.

SANDY
(Sarcastically)
Oh. And to what do I owe this most ... unexpected visit?

MRS. PATTON
I've come to get Karen's belongings.

SANDY
You've come to get Karen's belongings.

MRS. PATTON
I don't mean to impose. I did call but no one answered. I do want to get everything taken care of as soon as possible. I'm sure you understand.

SANDY
(To the air)
Ah, understanding. A great Patton trait.
(to MRS. PATTON)
I understand, Mrs. Patton, probably more than you realize.
(Seriously, almost compassionately)
I know there are some things you probably would like to have. Things Karen would want you to have. I have no intention of keeping those from you.

MRS PATTON

You have no intentions? My dear child, your intentions mean
nothing in this matter.

SANDY

Mrs. Patton, I haven't been a child in over twenty years. And so
far as my intentions. Well, let's just say, I have every intention
of seeing you to the door … now.

MRS. PATTON

I am not going without my daughter's belongings.

SANDY
(Trying to maintain her patience)
Mrs. Patton. I just got home. I haven't even been home since
… since it happened. And in three weeks, I have to have
everything packed up and moved out of here. That means
I'll have to go through everything. I promise, I will set aside
anything of Karen's you may …

MRS. PATTON
(Interrupting)
It has been over a week since Karen's death, and I do not
intend to let things go unsettled for another three weeks.

SANDY
(Losing patience)
What exactly is it you want?

MRS. PATTON

What ever belonged to Karen. Her clothes, jewelry, books,
dishes, linens.

SANDY
(Her sarcasm returns)
Oh, really? Well, let's see then ...
(Looking around the room, her gaze
settles on the dining room table.)
Ah ha.
(Picks up plate)
You want Karen's half of the dishes?
(She breaks the dish against the edge
of the table and hands half a plate to
MRS. PATTON.)
Here you go.

(She breaks the second plate in the
same manner and hands it to MRS.
PATTON also.)
And another.
(She grabs up half of the silverware on
the table and hands it to Mrs. Patton.)
These would be yours.
(She picks up a wine glass.)
Which part do you want, the cup or the stem?
(She breaks the glass against the table;
only the stem is left.)
I guess it's the stem. And the couch.
(She moves to the couch)
Now... which half would you prefer? I'll get the chain saw
and ...
(Makes sound of chainsaw)
...we'll divide all the furniture. The table, chairs, dresser. And
let's not forget the bed.

MRS. PATTON
Sandy ...

SANDY
And Karen's books.
(Taking books from the shelves, she
reads the titles then checks for Karen's
name inside as she hands them to
MRS. PATTON)
Let's see...Lesbian Woman... Our Right to Love. Sappho's
Citizens...Sapphic Songs...Wait. This one's mine.

MRS. PATTON
(As SANDY replaces the last book
on the shelf, MRS. PATTON drops
everything)
There is no reason to turn this into a fiasco.

SANDY
(Angrily)
A fiasco? I thought we already did that. Last week. Friday
night to be exact.

MRS. PATTON
You were creating a disturbance.

SANDY
You had hospital security remove me from Karen's room.

MRS. PATTON
She was in intensive care. She couldn't have visitors.

SANDY
(Angrily)
I'm not a visitor. Damn it! If Bobby hadn't called, I wouldn't
even have known where she was. I'd still be sitting here ...
waiting.

MRS. PATTON
He called against my wishes.

SANDY
Thank God your son doesn't listen to your wishes.

MRS. PATTON
(Angrily)
Who are you to thank God? Look at this. The way you live.
These books. I prayed to God to forgive you.

SANDY
Just me, Mrs. Patton? Well, maybe that was your mistake.

MRS. PATTON
(Coolly)
I just want what is rightfully mine.
(The two women look hard at each
other. It is SANDY who finally turns
away.)

SANDY
(Mostly to herself)
Damn it's cold in here.
(Picks up flashlight; quietly)
You can't just come in here and expect to divide up five years.
This is mine. That's hers. You can't do it that way. All of this
is what we had, the two of us.
(Starts to exit through basement door)
I don't think you'll find many memories here, Mrs. Patton.
None you'll want anyway.

(SANDY exits through basement
door leaving MRS. PATTON in the
midst of broken plates and scattered
books. For the first time her demeanor
eases, and she shows the cold of the
room and her loss. She picks up the
broken dishes at her feet and sets
them on the table, then gathers the
fallen books. The proper matron has
been replaced by an elderly woman.
As she sets the books on the desk, her
gaze falls on the photo of Sandy and
Karen camping together. She starts to
reach for it when SANDY enters from
the basement. MRS. PATTON turns
quickly from the photo and she and
SANDY meet head-on. They hesitate
in front of each other before MRS.
PATTON turns away. The demeanor
of a proper woman has returned.
SANDY exits to the kitchen to put a
teakettle on to boil. When she returns,
MRS. PATTON is sitting at one end of
the couch.

SANDY

I see you've decided which half of the couch you want.
(MRS. PATTON does not respond.)
I put some water on to boil … if you want some coffee or tea.
(No response)
Cocoa maybe.
(Still nothing and SANDY's discomfort
begins to show.)
Have you seen a cat around here? I can't seem to find Mr. C.
He usually comes when I call.

MRS. PATTON

I believe it's upstairs, under a bed.

SANDY

Thanks.
(SANDY exits to upstairs bedroom.
MRS. PATTON's attention slowly
returns to the photo on the desk. She
goes to it and picks it up.)

SANDY

(Entering from upstairs bedroom)
You're right. I think he's pretty mad at me for leaving him
alone.
(Noticing MRS. PATTON)
That's a good picture of her.
(No response)
It was taken last June, on that river trip we took in Idaho.
Shit, it was beautiful up there. I almost had Karen talked into
moving to Twin Falls.

MRS. PATTON'

(Replacing picture)
Karen would never have moved to Idaho.

                    SANDY
You're right. Too much country. Not enough traffic.
                    (Teakettle whistles)
Shit. There's the water.
                    (Hurrying to kitchen)
Want anything?

                    (There is no response and SANDY
                    sticks her head back into the living
                    room.)
Mrs. Patton?

                    (No answer)
I'll make some tea.

                    (SANDY exits to the kitchen.)

                    (MRS. PATTON returns to the photo
                    and studies it briefly before returning
                    to her place on the couch.)

                    (SANDY enters with a steaming pot
                    and two cups on a tray. She sets them
                    down on the coffee table.)

                    SANDY
Tea, Mrs. Patton?

The Party

Cast of Characters

Mickey Walker	female, mid-thirties
Maxine Ingram	female, mid-thirties
Carol Ann Jeffers	female, mid-thirties, Maxine's sister and a housewife
Kevin Walker	male, mid-twenties
Scott	male, effeminate, mid-twenties
Joan	female, mid-thirties
Diane	female, mid-thirties
Pat	female, mid-thirties
Guest 1	female, mid-thirties
Guest 2	female, mid-thirties

ACT I

THE SETTING is the home of
MICKEY WALKER and MAXINE
INGRAM. It is the living room that
takes up most of center stage. To stage
right, a divider separates the living
space from the kitchen. On the other
side of the living room, the front door
leads to the porch and the few shrubs
that surround it. There is also a back
door that exits from the kitchen and
a doorway near center stage that
leads to the hall and bedrooms. The
furnishings are essentially middle
class and include the basics – couch,
coffee table, living room chairs with
end tables, stereo/television, bookcase,
a table and chairs in the kitchen. It
is the condiments in the house, the
books and knickknacks on the almost
too full shelves, the newspapers
and magazines on the tables, the
paintings and photographs on the
wall (including Tee Corrine's solarized
photo of women making love), that
indicate to us that Mickey and Max
are not just roommates, but lovers.

SCENE 1

AT RISE: It is early evening. The
house is empty, its occupants
obviously gone for the evening.
CAROL ANN JEFFERS enters from
stage left and moves to the porch
carrying two suitcases, her purse
and a shopping bag stuffed full. She
juggles her load up onto the porch and
sets the suitcases down. She knocks,

but there is no answer. She rings the
doorbell with no response. She peers
in the window and raps on it.

> CAROL ANN
> (Calling)

Anybody home?

> (Examining the porch, she sees the
> mailbox on the porch post. She glances
> around to make sure she isn't being
> watched, swings the box to one side
> and reveals the house key behind it.
> She opens the door and sticks her
> head in.)

> CAROL ANN

Yoo hoo. anybody home? Maxine, are you here? Anybody?

> (Satisfied no one is home, she replaces
> the key and puts her suitcases inside,
> closing the door behind her. She turns
> the light on and looks around the
> room.)

> CAROL ANN

Well, Maxine, I sure hope I'm not messing up any of your
plans. But Mama always said blood's thicker than water.

> (Looking around)

Doesn't look like you've done too badly, baby sister.

> (She looks at a bookcase obviously
> reading titles then stands in front
> of the Tee Corrine photograph as if
> trying to figure it out. She shuffles and
> straightens newspapers on the coffee
> table then goes into the kitchen.)

Black out.

SCENE 2

When lights come up again, it is
several hours later. Only CAROL
ANN'S shopping bag remains in
the living room. Neither she nor
her suitcases are visible. The living
room light still burns. MAXINE and
MICKEY enter, approaching the
porch, perhaps through the audience.
They are still "high" from an evening
on the town and their interactions are
playful.

MICKEY

I still want to know how you managed tickets. The Raving
Hags. Goddess, they were great. I thought they were all sold
out.

MAX

They were.

MICKEY

So how did you do it?

MAX

That, my dear, falls under the jurisdiction of a lover's
prerogative.

MICKEY

Oh, really? And what else does such a jurisdiction cover?

MAX

Anything I want it to.

MICKEY

Really, now. Well, the concert was a pretty good birthday
present . . . for a start.

MAX

For a start? What makes you think there's anything else?

182

MICKEY

You mean that's it?

MAX

A concert tonight and a party tomorrow. What else could you want? Anyway, you'll probably get plenty of presents at the party.

MICKEY
(Stops MAX at the foot of the porch steps)

Yeah, but I doubt they'll be offering what I had in mind.

MAX

My dear woman, I guess you'll just have to make a wish.

MICKEY

All right, then. I wish, I wish . . .
(Sees light on in living room)

Oh, shit.

MAX

That isn't exactly what I would have wished for.
(MICKEY pulls MAX to one side out of view on the living room window.)

Mickey, what the. . .

MICKEY
(Interrupting, whispering)

Shh! The light.

MAX

The light?

MICKEY
(Continues to whisper)

The light is on.

MAX
(Mimicking MICKEY whisper)
So the light is on. You probably forgot to turn it off when you left.

MICKEY
I didn't forget to turn it off. I distinctly remember. I grabbed my jacket, picked up my wallet, got the house key and . . . Max! Someone's been in the house!

MAX
Mickey, would you give me a break. You just forgot to turn the light off like you always do, that's all.

MICKEY
I didn't forget. Someone's been in the house . . .

>   (CAROL ANN enters the living room
>   from the hall and MICKEY sees her
>   silhouette through the window.)
. . . and he's still there!

MAX
Oh my goddess! Get down!
>   (MAX grabs MICKEY and pulls her
>   down behind the bushes.)

MICKEY
I told you someone had been in the house, but would you believe me? Nooo. Not until the guy almost walks out on us and then suddenly you're the Amazon Battalion pulling me from the jaws of the great male death.

MAX
Would you cut it out? Do you think he saw us?

MICKEY
I don't know. I don't think so.

MAX

Well, we've got to do something. He's probably already walked off with half our stuff.

MICKEY

Yeah, and it's probably my half, too.

MAX

Get serious.

MICKEY

Okay. Don't panic.

MAX

I'm not panicking.

MICKEY

Just stay calm.

MAX

I am calm.

MICKEY

We've got to think this through.
                    (MAX waits impatiently as MICKEY
                    figures out what to do.)
Okay. We better let the male authorities handle this one.

MAX

Bravo.

MICKEY

You stay here and keep an eye on the guy and I'll go across the street to Mrs. Simpson's and call the cops.

MAX

No way. I'm not staying here by myself. Not with some male or males unknown on the other side of that door.

MICKEY

All right, then. I'll stay here and you go call the cops.

MAX

Are you crazy? If I leave you here, you'll probably go and do something heroic . . . like trying to sneak up on the guy with a baseball bat.

MICKEY

Then what do you suggest?

MAX

We'll both go.

MICKEY

All right, then.

(The two women stand simultaneously. MAX starts to head away from the porch towards the audience while MICKEY hurries toward the back of the house and exits at rear of stage.)

MAX

Mickey!

(MAX changes directions, hurrying after MICKEY and exits at rear of stage. The back door of the kitchen opens and MICKEY enters slowly, baseball bat raised. She signals and MAX enters behind her.)

MAX
(Whispering)

This is crazy.

                    MICKEY
Shhhh.

                    (MICKEY creeps cautiously into the
                    living room and towards the hallway,
                    baseball bat still raised. MAXINE
                    follows reluctantly. They BOTH speak
                    in hushed voices.)

                    MAX
You're going to get us both killed.

                    MICKEY
Hush.

                    MAX
When I said we should both go, I meant to Mrs. Simpson's.

                    MICKEY
                    (Turns to face MAX, lowering bat)
If you don't shut up you're going to give us away.
                    (CAROL ANN enters from the hall,
                    unseen by MICKEY or MAX.)

                    CAROL ANN
Maxine, you're home!

                    (MICKEY spins around, bat ready to
                    strike.)

                    MAX
Mickey, no!

                    (MAX grabs the bat and pushes
                    MICKEY to one side then turns to
                    CAROL ANN in disbelief.)
Carol Ann?

                    CAROL ANN
                    (Hugging MAX)
Maxine. It's so good to see you.

                        187

MAX

Carol Ann. What are you . . .

CAROL ANN
(Oblivious to both MAXINE'S
confusion and to MICKEY'S existence)

It's been such a long time. How are you?

MAX

But how did you . . .

CAROL ANN

You are looking good. Must be that California sunshine.

MAX

But . . .

CAROL ANN

I hope you don't mind. No one was home, so I just let myself in. I knew you would hide the key where Mama always did.

MICKEY

On a little nail behind the mail box?

(CAROL ANN notices MICKEY
for the first time. As they introduce
themselves, MAX appears distracted
by her surroundings.)

MICKEY
(Shaking CAROL ANN'S hand)

Hi. I'm Mickey Walker, Max's . . .

                    MAX
            (Suddenly aware of what is about to
            be said, interrupting)
Housemate. Mickey's my housemate. Aren't you, Mickey?
            (MICKEY looks at MAXINE,
            surprised by her declaration. As
            CAROL ANN proceeds through her
            recitation explaining her sudden
            appearance, MAX begins fidgeting
            with the furnishings of her home.
            She straightens the magazines on
            the coffee table, then slips several
            into a table drawer. She picks up a
            handful of newspapers and quickly
            stuffs several of them under the couch
            cushion. As MAX continues hiding
            Lesbian publications and knickknacks,
            MICKEY listens to CAROL ANN, but
            only halfheartedly. She is distracted
            by MAXINE'S activity.)

                CAROL ANN
I sure hope I'm not inconveniencing you or anything.

                 MICKEY
Ah, no. Not at all.

                CAROL ANN
I know my showing up here is sudden and all, but the
opportunity came up and Bobby said, 'Honey, you just got
to go and visit your sister.' Bobby's my husband, but I guess
you know that.
            (MAX has gone to the bookcase and
            is selectively turning books, binding
            down, so the titles do not show.
            MICKEY continues to watch with
            curious disbelief.)

                 MICKEY
I'm glad you got the chance to come.

                    189

CAROL ANN

He's the regional manager for Cooper's Seed and Supply and gets to travel a lot so I guess he thought it was my turn to do a little traveling. I bet he's sorry the boys didn't get to come with me. We've got two.

MICKEY
(Watches MAX staring at the Tee Corrine print)
Really? Sounds interesting.
(To MAX, as she starts to reach for the print)
Max, what are you doing?

MAX
(Startled, she turns quickly from the print to the coffee table and straightens the newspapers, again)
Straightening. Just straightening up, that's all.

CAROL ANN
(To MAX)
No need to do that on my account, Maxine. If I haven't noticed a little dirt by now, I'm sure not going to. This is a lovely little house. I bet rent here is terrible.
(MAX tries to intercede on MICKEY'S answer, but isn't fast enough.)

MICKEY
We own it.

CAROL ANN
You do? Both of you?

MICKEY
Three years, now.

MAX
A lot of single people buy homes together out here.

CAROL ANN

Really? Well, I guess it is expensive to live by yourself nowadays. I guess that's one of the advantages of marriage. At least you don't have to worry about all of that.

MAX

Carol Ann, I suppose you'll be wanting to get settled in somewhere . . . before it gets too late?

CAROL ANN

Actually, I was hoping we'd sit up and talk . . . like we used to.
(To MICKEY)
Daddy would always end up hollering at us to turn the lights out and go to sleep.

MAX

You were?

CAROL ANN
(To MAX)
But I'm just too tired. I'd probably fall asleep in the middle of one of your stories and never get to hear the end of it. So, if you don't mind, I'll just turn in.

MAX

Here?

CAROL ANN

Or where ever you'd rather have me sleep. I put my bags in the bedroom on the left. I hope that's okay.

MICKEY

No problem that's . . .
(Simultaneously with MAX)
. . . the guest room.

MAX
(Simultaneously with MICKEY)
Mickey's room.
(Continuing)
It's Mickey's room, but we use it for guests. Mickey and I kind
of bunk together when we have guests.

MICKEY
(Mouthing words to MAX)
Bunk together?

CAROL ANN
Well, I won't have any of that while I'm here. Mickey, you just
stay in your room. Maxine and I will be fine together.
(To MAX)
It'll be just like old times when we were kids.
(To MICKEY)
We're used to it.
(CAROL ANN exits down hall.)

MICKEY
So was I.

MAX
Well, I guess I'll get ready for bed, too.
(She starts to exit.)

MICKEY
Get your butt back here, Maxine Ingram. Just what in goddess'
name is going on here?

MAX
What do you mean, exactly?

                    MICKEY
What do I mean . . . exactly?
                    (Pulls newspapers from under couch
                    cushion)
I mean newspapers under cushions . . .
                    (Pulls magazines from the drawer and
                    drops them onto the coffee table)
. . . magazines shoved into drawers . . .

                    MICKEY
                    (Continuing, goes to bookcase)
. . . books turned down so you can't see their titles. For a
moment there, I thought you were going to take the pictures
off the wall.

                      MAX
                    (Reaching for the Tee Corrine print)
Good idea.

                    MICKEY

Max!

                    (MAXINE leaves the picture where it
                    is and turns to MICKEY.)

                      MAX
She's my sister, Mickey. My only sister.

                    MICKEY
I'm your lover.

                      MAX
Shhhh.

                    MICKEY
Maxine, we've got a problem.

                      MAX
I know. What am I going to do, Mickey?

                    MICKEY
Tell her.

                         MAX
Yeah, but what?

                        MICKEY
                      (Impatiently)
That you're a d . . .

                         MAX
                (Putting her fingers to MICKEY'S lips
                to quiet her)
Shhhh!

                        MICKEY
                   (Lowers her voice)
That you're a dyke. What else would you tell her?

                         MAX
                      (Quietly)
I don't know, but I can't tell her that.
                    (MICKEY throws up her hands in
                    despair. They continue talking in
                    hushed terms.)

                         MAX
She's my sister.

                        MICKEY
And?

                         MAX
And I always looked up to her . . . wanted to be like her. I
idolized her when we were little. I can't tell her about us. She
wouldn't understand.

                        MICKEY
You want to be like her, now? Happily married to what's his
face . . . Billy? With two little miniature males clinging to your
knees? Is that what you want?

                         MAX
Bobby.

                              MICKEY
What?

                               MAX
His name is Bobby.

                              MICKEY
Same difference.

                               MAX
Anyway, that's not the point.

                              MICKEY
You're right. The point is we have an understanding. More
than that, we have an agreement. We are out. That's it. Pure
and simple. To mom, dad, the chief of police and Mrs. Simpson
across the street. We are not hiding, from the neighbors, our
employers or our relatives.

                               MAX
I never thought anyone would just show up on the doorstep.
I always thought they'd call or write, I'd tell them and they'd
decide not to come.

                              MICKEY
Well, it didn't work out that way, did it? She didn't call. She
didn't write. She's here, now, and you haven't told her. This
isn't a minor disagreement to me. This is how we decided to
live our lives.

                           CAROL ANN
                    (Entering from the hallway)
Oops. "Family" discussion?

                               MAX
                    (Relieved to be interrupted)
No. Come in. Please.

MICKEY

I'd better get my things out of . . .
(Sarcastically to MAX)
. . . *your* bedroom.

CAROL ANN

Mickey? Your name isn't short for Maxine, is it?

MICKEY

Yeah, it is.

CAROL ANN

I bet that's confusing to your friends, you two living together
and all.

MICKEY

No, only to me.
(To MAX)
And don't forget tomorrow.
(She exits through hallway.)

CAROL ANN

Is Mickey upset about something?

MAX

Just a little misunderstanding, that's all.

CAROL ANN

I hope it's not about my being here.
(MAX doesn't respond)
It means a lot to me to be able to come here like this, I mean
without so much as a call or anything. I know we haven't seen
much of each other these past few years, but you've always
been special to me. I've always been kind of proud of the way
you moved all the way out here and put yourself through
college and all.

MAX

(Preoccupied, not really attending to
what CAROL ANN is saying)
It's no big deal.

CAROL ANN

It is to me.

MAX

You could've done it.

CAROL ANN

No way! Not me. Bobby and I were already planning on getting married before we even got out of high school. We really were too young, but you couldn't tell us that. Lord knows, Mama and Daddy tried. And then the boys came along. Well, that's all water under the bridge, as they say.
(Pausing, continues)
I'm going on to bed. You coming?

MAX

In a little while.

CAROL ANN

Good night, then.
(Starts to exit)
Maxine . . . thanks.

(CAROL ANN exits through hallway. MAX stares after her. She looks around the room then studies the Tee Corrine print on the wall. Finally, she resigns herself to a seat on the couch as lights fall.)

SCENE 3

AT RISE: It is early the next morning.
Every hint of Lesbian paraphernalia
has been removed from the house.
The bookcase and tabletops are near
empty. Ladies Home Journal, Readers'
Digest and other such magazines are
neatly arranged on the coffee table.
And a "cute" poster of kittens and
puppies adorns the wall where the
Corrine print had hung. MAX sits at
the kitchen table reading the daily
paper and drinking coffee when
MICKEY enters from the hall.

                    MICKEY
          (Startled by the new decor)
Whoa!
          (Surveying the room slowly)
Who's our new decorator, Jerry Falwell?

                    MAX
Good morning to you, too.

                    MICKEY
          (Examining the kitten/puppy poster)
Where did you find this treasure?

                    MAX
Mrs. Simpson loaned it to us.

                    MICKEY
Us? Really?
          (She picks up a crocheted poodle
          covering a roll of toilet paper.)

Cute. How did your sister do on this midnight scavenger
hunt?

MAX

Is this going to go on all day?

MICKEY
(Getting a cup of coffee, takes seat
across from MAX)

Actually, I figured you had something like this in mind before
I even got up this morning. I think it was all the banging,
rattling and dragging I heard last night. So, what do you have
planned for the party tonight? How about a rousing game of
Old Maid? I believe most of us should qualify.

MAX

They're our friends. They'll understand. A lot better than you
do, probably.

MICKEY

Ah, yes. Come into my closet, said the het to the dyke. They'll
love it.

CAROL ANN
(Entering from the hall)

Good morning, everyone.

MICKEY

Good morning, Carol Ann. And how did you sleep last
night?

CAROL ANN

Like a log. I didn't even hear Maxine come to bed.

MICKEY

Really?
(Sarcastically to MAX)

Neither did I.

MAX
(Puts the paper down forcefully,
speaks to MICKEY)

Carol Ann, would you like some coffee?

                    CAROL ANN
Don't bother. I can get it.
                    (Picking up the coffee pot)
How about my warming yours up, Mickey?

                    MICKEY
                    (Holding out her cup for CAROL
                    ANN to top off)
Ah, now maybe that's the answer.
                    (MAX glares at MICKEY.)

                    CAROL ANN
Maxine?

                    MAX
No, thank you.

                    (To MICKEY, as she stands)
I've had enough.

                    (MAX exits the hall. CAROL ANN
                    takes her chair at the table.)

                    CAROL ANN
You two must know each other real well. It seems like you're
always saying things to each other I don't understand.

                    MICKEY
I thought we did. Look, I'm sorry. We really shouldn't be
carrying on like this. It's not fair to you.

                    CAROL ANN
It's okay. Married people do it a lot, too. Bobby and I do,
anyway. Sometimes, though, what's not being said isn't being
said at all. And what you think is being said keeps you from
hearing what's really going on. Know what I mean?

                    MICKEY
Boy, do I ever.

CAROL ANN

So, even when you think you're hearing what's not being said, it's really better to ask and get it said out loud. Then you know for sure. Unless, what's being said out loud isn't the truth, either.

MICKEY

It can hurt, too . . . finding out what you thought was true isn't true after all.

CAROL ANN

It can rip you clean apart, that's for sure.
                    (Pauses, then stands)
Well, why don't I scramble us some eggs. You've got eggs, don't you?

MICKEY

You don't have to do that.

CAROL ANN

It's no trouble. It'll help me feel at ease. I'm always more comfortable when I'm making myself useful.

MICKEY

All right, then. Scrambled eggs it is.

CAROL ANN
                    (Begins fixing breakfast)
Tell me about tonight.

MICKEY

Tonight?

CAROL ANN

You've got plans, haven't you? Isn't that what you and Maxine have been talking about?

MICKEY

Sort of. It's my birthday and . . .

CAROL ANN
(Interrupting)
Your birthday? No wonder you're concerned. If you've got
plans for your birthday, don't let me mess them up.

MICKEY
We were just going to have a few friends over.

CAROL ANN
Well, if you think I'll be in the way, you just tell me. I can
always stay back in the bedroom.

MICKEY
Right now, I think you would be more of an asset than Max.

CAROL ANN
Now, that's silly. I don't even know your friends.
(MAX enters from hall and gets
another cup of coffee.)

CAROL ANN
Maxine, how many eggs do you want scrambled?

MAX
(Sitting down)
None for me, please.

CAROL ANN
It's not good to start the day without breakfast. I always make
Bobby and the boys eat a good breakfast.

MICKEY
She's right, you know. Two eggs all around for everyone . . .
except for me. I'm on my way out.
(Quietly, to MAX)
The time is right. Trust me, Max.

MAX
You don't know what you're talking about.

MICKEY

Yes, I do. Do it.
                        (To CAROL ANN)
And I promise, I'll stop for breakfast first thing.
                        (Stops at front door to survey the
                        newly decorated premises once more)
What can I say. Such talent.
                        (She exits through front door.)

MAX
                        (Ignoring MICKEY'S last comment)
So, Carol Ann, how are the boys doing?

CAROL ANN

They're getting so big, Maxine, you'd never know them. Freddie will be in fourth grade this year and Bobby Junior's already acting like he's in high school, and he's not even twelve, yet.

MAX

I guess they do grow up fast.

CAROL ANN

They sure do. All Bobby Junior can talk about is what kind of car he wants when he's sixteen and what he's going to do when he gets out of high school. I just hope he doesn't get himself married right off the bat like his father did.

MAX

His father did okay. I mean, isn't he?

CAROL ANN

Oh, Bobby couldn't be better. He's got this job that lets him travel . . . across six states. I mean, he's gone half the time. He's supposed to be gone to a convention in Dallas right now, but he's home with the boys, I guess. Aren't you working today?

MAX

No. I took a couple of days off. Ah, Carol Ann . . .

CAROL ANN

For Mickey's birthday?

(MAX looks a CAROL ANN in
surprise.)

What's going on tonight? You've got a party planned, don't
you?

MAX

We're just having a few friends over, that's all. Listen, Carol
Ann . . .

CAROL ANN

That's what Mickey said, but there's more to it than that.
You know, Maxine, good friends are hard to come by. The
last thing I would want to do is come between you and your
friends. Why don't I just get lost for the evening.? I could
go to a movie or something. I haven't been to a movie since,
well since . . . I guess *Paint Your Wagon* was the last movie we
went to. You ever see *Paint Your Wagon*? That sure was a great
movie, wasn't it?

MAX

It was okay, I guess. What I was going to say . . .

CAROL ANN

I always loved going to the movies. You go to movies very
much?

MAX

Yes, but . . .

CAROL ANN

Well, maybe that's what I'll do, go to the movies, tonight.

MAX

Carol Ann, please! Would you just listen?

CAROL ANN

What is it, Maxine?

                              MAX
I have to tell you something.

                          CAROL ANN
All right, then. I'm listening.
                              (There is a long silence while MAX
                              hems and haws, starting to speak and
                              then hesitating. She stands and paces
                              nervously as she tries to find the right
                              words.)

Well?
                              (MAX gestures to CAROL ANN to
                              wait as she continues to stumble for
                              words.)

                              MAX
This isn't easy. I mean, I've thought about telling you, even
picked up the phone to call you . . .

                          CAROL ANN
So . . . ?

                              MAX
                          (Haltingly)
I just didn't want to hurt you . . . I didn't know how you would
take it . . .

                          CAROL ANN
Maxine, just say it.

                              MAX
                    (Continues to hesitate, stumble)
Well . . . it's just that . . . well . . . I'm . . .

                          CAROL ANN
                    (Drops the spatula into the frying pan)
Oh, my god!
                    (She grabs Max by the shoulders)
You're dying, aren't you?

                               205

                    MAX
                 (Confused)
What?

                 CAROL ANN
Oh, god, what is it? Cancer? Leukemia? A brain tumor?

                    MAX
No, no. It's nothing like that.

                 CAROL ANN
                 (Hugs MAX)
Oh, my god, Maxine. I'm so sorry.

                    MAX
Carol Ann, I'm not dying!

                 CAROL ANN
           (Holds MAX a arms length)
You're not?

                    MAX
No, I'm not.

                 CAROL ANN
Thank god. Then what is it you wanted to tell me?

                    MAX
Well, it's, it's . . . Mickey.

                 CAROL ANN
She's dying?

                    MAX
No! She's . . .

                 CAROL ANN
Well, then, who is dying?

MAX

Nobody's dying!

(MICKEY enters through the
back door as MAX makes this last
declaration.)

MICKEY

Who's dying?

MAX
(Throwing up her hands in defeat)

I am.

(To CAROL ANN, quickly,
reassuringly)

Just kidding.

MICKEY
(Somewhat bewildered)
Don't mean to barge back in, but I forgot a couple of books.
(Notices CAROL ANN'S
bewilderment as she goes to the book
case)
Carol Ann? Are you okay?

CAROL ANN
I don't know. I've never been so confused in my life.
(MICKEY looks to MAX, but MAX just
shrugs her shoulders. MICKEY checks
titles of books in the bookcase.)

CAROL ANN
If you don't mind, I think I'll go back to bed for a while. Are
you sure you're all right, Maxine?

MAX

Yes, I'm fine.

CAROL ANN

Good. I'm so very glad to hear that.
(CAROL ANN exits down hall.
MICKEY returns to the kitchen empty
handed and turns to MAX for an
explanation.)

MICKEY

You didn't tell her, did you?

MAX

I thought you were going over to Paula's this morning.

MICKEY

I forgot the books or didn't you hear? Anyway, that's not the
issue. Why didn't you tell her?

MAX

I tried. But she thought I was telling her I was dying.

MICKEY

Dyking, Max, dyking. You were supposed to tell her you are
dyking, not dying.

MAX
(In a hushed voice)
That is so easy for you to say. You had it so much easier.

MICKEY

What do you mean, easier?

MAX

Your brother had already come out to your family when you
finally told them. He had softened them up for you.

MICKEY

Oh, yeah. Like my mom was overjoyed when I told her,
"Congratulations, Mom. You lucked out. Two-thirds of your
kids are queer."

MAX
(Through gritted teeth)
Would you keep your voice down?

MICKEY
And my sexuality and my spirituality and my politics, no
doubt. Anything else you would like me to keep down?
(MICKEY and MAX glare at each
other.)

MICKEY
Oh, yeah, about the books. In which closet will I find Lesbian
Ethics?

Black out.

ACT II

SCENE 1

It is later that day, less than an hour
before the party is to get under way.
The house has been decorated for the
upcoming event in pink and white
streamers and balloons. Bottles of
liquid refreshment and eating utensils
cover the kitchen table and bowls of
nuts sit on tables in the living room.
There is a touch to the premises that is
far too feminine.

KEVIN, MICKEY'S brother, and his
lover, SCOTT, enter onto the porch.
Both are dressed in jeans and tee shirts
and KEVIN carries a box wrapped in
lavender paper and ribbon. KEVIN
knocks at the door then opens it
slightly.

                    KEVIN
                (Calling)
Mickey? Maxine? It's Kevin. Mind if two boys enter your
abode?
                (Seeing the decorations, he swings the
                door open.)
Yo, Scott, get a load of this.
                (SCOTT sticks his head through the
                door and gazes at the decorations.)

                    SCOTT
Whoa. Something's happened here, Kev. You think maybe
aliens got them?

                    MICKEY
              (Leaning out from hallway)
Kevin. Scott. Come on in. I'll be right there.
                    (As MICKEY retreats into the hall,
                    KEVIN and SCOTT enter. They both
                    wander about the room eyeing the
                    decorations and new decor with much
                    disbelief and trepidation.)

                    SCOTT
              (Pausing in front of the kitten/puppy
              poster, sarcastically)
Hey, Kev. This is just the poster I've been wanting for our
bedroom.

                    MICKEY
              (Enters from the hall, tying a bathrobe
              around her; sarcastic, hard, almost
              bitter)
You want it, Scott? I'll let you have it . . . real cheap.

                    SCOTT
              (Backs away from the poster and
              MICKEY)
Hey, no problem, Mickey. Its, ah . . . nice.
                    (SCOTT continues examining the
                    room as KEVIN and MICKEY greet
                    each other.)

                    KEVIN
              (Hugging MICKEY)
Happy birthday, Sis. We thought we'd drop by and give you
this before your guests arrive and turn this into no man's
land.

                    SCOTT
Definitely before your guests arrive.

                    MICKEY
              (Shrugging off SCOTT'S sarcasm;
               takes present from KEVIN)
Thanks, Kev. Should I open it now or wait till later?

                    KEVIN
Wait and open it with the rest of your presents. I promise it
won't embarrass you.

                    SCOTT
              (Picks up crocheted poodle)
Speaking of embarrassment.
                    (Tips it in her direction)
Cute.

                    KEVIN
Yeah, what's with the pink and white, anyway?

                    MICKEY
              (Shaking her head)
It's a long story, and I'm in a rotten mood.

                    SCOTT
Yo, hear that, Kev? Long story . . . rotten mood. We're out of
here.
                    (SCOTT heads for the door.)

                    KEVIN
              (To SCOTT, stopping him before he
               exits)
Hang on a minute.
              (To MICKEY)
Are you all right?

                    MICKEY
Yeah, it's just that . . .

                    MAX
                    (Enters from the hall, interrupting
                    MICKEY; coolly)
Kevin . . . Scott.

                    (Stops suddenly; looks from KEVIN to
                    SCOTT and back again; friendlier)
Kevin. Scott.

                    (Smiles wryly; excitedly)
Kevin and Scott! Yes!

                    SCOTT
Don't worry, Max, we're not staying.

                    KEVIN
We just stopped by to wish my kid sister a happy birthday
and then we're gone.

                    MAX
Gone? There's no need to rush off! The party will be starting
soon.
                    (KEVIN and SCOTT look at MAX and
                    then each other in disbelief.)

                    MICKEY
                    (With disbelief)
MAX?!

                    MAX
Maybe you could call a few of your friends to join us?

                    SCOTT
Ke-vin, I think we had better get out of here.

                    MICKEY
                    (To MAX)
What are you talking about?

                    MAX
                    (To know one in particular)
Yeah, that's it. The boys can stay and if they invite some of
their friends . . .

MICKEY
(Finishing for her)
Our friends won't step foot inside that front door. Are you
listening to yourself?

SCOTT
(To KEVIN)
Is she making fun of us again?

MICKEY
(To SCOTT)
She doesn't make fun of you. She just puts you in your place.
(To MAX)
Max, this is crazy!

MAX
Of course it isn't.
(Pulls MICKEY to one side)
This could be the answer to our prayers.

MICKEY
Two gay guys are the answer to our prayers?

MAX
If there are males in the room, Carol Ann will be less likely to
figure it out.

MICKEY
If there are males in the room, I won't be able to figure it out.

SCOTT
Kevin, lets get going while the getting's good.
(He starts for the door.)

MAX
Scott Taylor! You stay right where you are. You owe me.

MICKEY
Max, wait a minute.

KEVIN

Yeah, Max. Wait a minute.

SCOTT

What do you mean I *owe* you?

MAX

Remember last winter, when you two went skiing?

KEVIN

Tried to go skiing is more like it.

MAX
(To KEVIN)

Exactly.

(To SCOTT)

You blew a water hose, over heated your engine and cracked your block. And instead of paying through the nose to some roadside-rip-off, who did you call?

SCOTT

Yeah, but . . .

MAX
(To SCOTT)

And who drove up on her weekend off to tow you two home so you wouldn't freeze to death by the side of the road.

SCOTT
(To KEVIN)

I told you freezing would have been better.

MAX
(To KEVIN)

And when you bought Scott a new puppy three days before you left on your anniversary cruise, who kept it for you . . . even though it wasn't house broken <u>and</u> had a penchant for the leather of new Birkenstocks?

                         KEVIN
I paid for your shoes.

                          MAX
That's not the point.

                        MICKEY
Exactly, Max. The point is, this is a dyke party. What are we
supposed to tell our friends when they show up and find
these two prancing around?

                         SCOTT
Now *she's* making fun of us.

                          MAX
We won't have to tell them anything. The boys will do it.

                         KEVIN
We will?

                          MAX
When women arrive, they'll show them to the bedroom . . .

                         SCOTT
Oh, Lord have mercy . . .

                          MAX
                     (Continuing)
. . . where they can leave their coats. And while they are in the
bedroom, they'll simply tell our friends our predicament . . .

                        MICKEY
Your predicament.

                          MAX
                     (Continuing)
. . . so everyone will understand before they even join the
party.

SCOTT
(To KEVIN)
You hear that, Kevin? You hear that? They want us to take a
bunch of raging, radical dykes into the bedroom and tell them
. . . tell them . . .
(To MICKEY and MAX)
Tell them what?

MICKEY
(Angrily)
Tell them that my lover, with whom I thought I had an honest,
aboveboard, no hidden agenda relationship refuses to tell her
sister that she is a dyke!

KEVIN
Is that what this is all about?

MICKEY
(To KEVIN)
You're damn straight!

SCOTT
I hope not!
(To MAX)
Look, Maxine, you're right. You have been a wonderful,
unselfish, self-sacrificing . . .

MICKEY
What?

                    SCOTT
                 (Continuing)
... giving! I mean giving ... friend to two totally undeserving,
worthless, despicable, sniveling, totally selfish males . . . and
we do owe you . . . oh, what we owe you . . . and we . . .
                 (Sees KEVIN'S look of total dismay)
... I would love to help you out of this predicament . . . but
just look at us . . .
                 (Moves next to KEVIN)
... we simply are not dressed for a party.
                 (MAX stands next to the two boys and
                 eyes them up and down, sizing them up.)

                    MAX
No problem. You can borrow something of mine. And Mickey
has some jackets, too.

                    SCOTT
Kevin, this is definitely too much.

                    CAROL ANN
                 (Entering through back door, grocery
                 bag in arms)
Yoo-hoo.
                 (Everyone in the living room stops
                 cold. CAROL ANN sets the bag down
                 on a kitchen chair.)
Sorry it took so long, but I couldn't find the olives. You know
how it is trying to shop some place you've never been before.
                 (Enters living room and sees KEVIN
                 and SCOTT for the first time)
Oh, my goodness. The guests are arriving and I still have to
change.
                 (She exits hurriedly through the hall,
                 leaving the other four in the living
                 room to stare at each other.)

                    MICKEY
                 (Mimicking *Poltergeist*)
She's ba-a-a---ack.
                 Black out.

                      218

SCENE 2

It is 7:30 that evening, just about time for guests to start arriving. MICKEY and MAX, dressed in dyke party apparel, putter about the kitchen, putting food onto trays and trays onto the table. KEVIN enters from the hall and stops just inside living room. He is dressed in his same jeans, but with a nice shirt, men's sport jacket and tie. Hearing him enter, MICKEY goes over to him.

KEVIN

What do you think?

MICKEY
(She straightens KEVIN'S shirt collar and tie.)
Not bad. Your mother's daughter sure has great taste.

KEVIN

Yeah? Well, I wish your mother's son had more sense than to be here.

MICKEY

You don't have to stay, Kevin.

KEVIN

What you don't understand, Mickey, is that you may have chosen to live with Max, but, since you have, Scott and I have to live *in spite* of her.

MICKEY

Where is Scott?

KEVIN

Still in the bathroom, I guess . . . unless he's gone out the window.

219

                    MICKEY
Did he find something to wear?

                    KEVIN
I guess so.

                    MICKEY
What about Carol Ann?

                    KEVIN
I assumed she had something to wear.

                    MICKEY
You know what I mean.

                    KEVIN
Probably waiting for Scott to get out of the bathroom.
                    (Suddenly, SCOTT makes an entrance
                    from the hallway. Dressed in an
                    evening dress, elbow high gloves,
                    garish rhinestone necklace and
                    bracelet and balancing in high heels
                    obviously too small for him, he sways
                    teetering across the living room,
                    surprising KEVIN and MICKEY.)

                    KEVIN
Scott!

                    MICKEY
Oh, goddess!

                    (MAX looks up from her activity in
                    the kitchen and drops the dish in her
                    hands.)

                    CAROL ANN
                    (Calling from hallway, off stage)
Maxine? Do you have any perfume I could borrow?
                    (MICKEY and KEVIN grab SCOTT
                    by the arms and rush him toward the
                    front door.)

                    MICKEY
            (Shouting to CAROL ANN)
Look on top of the dresser in our . . .
            (Directs last part more to MAX)
. . . in Max-*ine's* bedroom!
                    (MICKEY and KEVIN rush SCOTT
                    out the front door and onto the porch
                    as three of the guests, JOAN, DIANE
                    and PAT, arrive dressed to party and
                    bearing gifts. As SCOTT grabs a porch
                    post for support, KEVIN falls against
                    the house in a fit of laughter. The three
                    guests stop in their tracks and stare.)

                    MAX
            (Still in kitchen, yells)
Mickey!!

                    (MICKEY looks at her guests, shrugs
                    her shoulders, and takes one last look
                    at SCOTT and hurries to the kitchen
                    closing the front door behind her.)

                    SCOTT
            (To the guests)
Hi. I'm your gay guy guide for the evening, Greg.
                    (KEVIN bursts into another fit of
                    laughter.)

                    MAX
            (As MICKEY rushes into the kitchen)
What does he think he's doing?

                    MICKEY
Getting even maybe?

                    CAROL ANN
                    (Entering from hall, goes to kitchen)
Maxine? Mickey? Is everything all right?
                    (Seeing dish of food on floor)
Oh, my goodness! What happened here?
                    (CAROL ANN gets down on her
                    hands and knees between MICKEY
                    and MAX and begins to pick up the
                    pieces. MICKEY and MAX stand over
                    her, staring eye-to-eye, then slowly
                    lower to the floor, their eye contact
                    never breaking. Each picks up one
                    piece of the dish. They rise slowly,
                    simultaneously, and put the pieces on
                    the table.)

                    MAX
                    (In a harsh whisper)
You love every minute of this, don't you?

                    MICKEY
                    (Also whispering)
I'm beginning to.

                    (MAX and MICKEY do not move as
                    CAROL ANN stands up between
                    them and sets pieces of the dish on
                    the table. She picks up a dish rag off
                    the table then bends back down and
                    continues cleaning up.)

KEVIN
(Composing himself enough to speak
to the guests)
Would you ladies please follow us?
(When the guests hesitate)
It's by special request . . . from the women of the house . . .
really.

(SCOTT leans on KEVIN and the
two awkwardly lead the entourage
through the front door and into
the living room. The guests gaze at
the decor, surprised by it and the
decorations.)

(MAX sees them. PAT starts to speak,
but MAX quickly signals her to be
quiet and frantically waves the troop
toward the hall. The three quests,
confused and bewildered, exit through
the hall after the boys.)

(CAROL ANN finishes cleaning up
the floor. MICKEY and MAX remain
in the same places they were when
CAROL ANN began cleaning. They
obviously do not let their eyes meet.)

CAROL ANN
(Standing)
There. No damage done and no hard feelings.
(Looking from MICKEY to MAX)
Right girls?

MICKEY
(Without heart)
Yeah, Carol Ann . . . sure.

                    CAROL ANN
                    (With revelry)
Then let's party hearty.
                    (CAROL ANN takes MAX by the
                    hand and, half dragging her along,
                    "dances" into the living room and
                    turns on a CD. Jazzy music fills the
                    room and CAROL ANN sways,
                    without much rhythm, as MAX stands
                    nearby.)

                    (MICKEY drifts into the living room
                    as PAT, DIANE and JOAN enter from
                    the hall. The three new arrivals are
                    still taken aback by the appearance
                    of the premises as well as whatever
                    they have been told by the boys in the
                    depths of the bedrooms.)

                    (PAT and JOAN go over to MICKEY,
                    wish her a happy birthday and hand
                    her gifts. MICKEY only half smiles,
                    thanks them and directs them into the
                    kitchen to the food and drink. DIANE
                    goes to one side of the living room,
                    near the poster of the kittens/puppies.
                    No one, with the exception of CAROL
                    ANN, is in a partying mood.)

                    DIANE
                    (Signaling MICKEY to come over)

Mickey!

                    (MICKEY goes reluctantly to DIANE,
                    head down as if approaching an
                    unavoidable punishment.)

MICKEY
(As she approaches DIANE)
I know . . . I know. It's heterosexist, dishonest, politically
incorrect . . . we had no right letting you walk into this without
telling you first . . . this is supposed to be a women-only
gathering and you were greeted by boys . . . in drag, yet.

DIANE
(Putting her arm around MICKEY'S
shoulders)
Actually, I was going to compliment you on the poster. You
know, my kid would love that? She would have these all
over the house if I didn't draw the line at her bedroom door.
What's going on here?
(Two more guests arrive at the front
door and ring the doorbell.)

SCOTT
(From hallway, off stage, calling)
I'll get it!

(MAX'S back stiffens. Conversation
ceases and all eyes but CAROL ANN'S
freeze on the hall entrance. SCOTT
enters, dressed in his jeans and a satin-
like shirt. Only a rhinestone bracelet
remains of his former attire. Everyone,
except CAROL ANN, watches intently
as he crosses the living room to the
door. KEVIN enters from hall and
stands in the hall doorway watching,
enjoying every moment.)

                    SCOTT
          (Opening the front door, he bows
          low and, with the hand wearing the
          bracelet, makes a grand sweep into the
          living room.)
Good evening. Won't you come in?
          (The two guests hesitate at the door
          then lean in to see if they are at the
          right place.)

                    DIANE
          (Waving to the guests)
Hi, Ladies. Come on in.
          (They wave back, smiling recognition,
          start toward her then hesitate just
          inside the door.)

                    SCOTT
          (Closing the door)
Let me show you where you can put your coats. Follow me,
please.
          (SCOTT heads for the hall, but the
          new arrivals still hesitate.)

                    DIANE
Go on. You'll love it.

          (The guests follow SCOTT. As they
          pass, MAX and MICKEY each gives
          a half-hearted, reticent smile to the
          women. SCOTT leads the guests,
          exiting into the hall. KEVIN starts to
          follow, but before he can, CAROL
          ANN comes up and takes his arm.)

                    CAROL ANN
          (Leading KEVIN back into living
          room)
There you are. I was wondering where you went. I didn't get
a chance to introduce myself earlier. I'm Carol Ann, Maxine's
sister.

So I've heard.

CAROL ANN
(Pleased)
Really? Oh. Well, look at that. You don't have a thing to eat or
drink. Let me show you where the food is.
> (As CAROL ANN guides KEVIN to
> the kitchen, he looks back and gives
> a wink and mischievous smile to
> MAX. She starts to follow, but DIANE
> intercepts her, putting her arm around
> MAX'S shoulders and pulling her
> in close. DIANE now has MAX and
> MICKEY both, an arm around each.)

DIANE
Well, girls . . . I can call you girls, can't I . . . you have definitely
out done yourselves. As parties go . . . this one takes the cake
. . . there will be cake later won't there? Tell me, which of you
is going to jump out of it?

Black out

SCENE 3

It is an hour and a half or so later.
The house looks much the same.
There is less food and a few cups and
plates are sitting around, but basically
very little partying has taken place.
JOAN and a couple of guests sit on
the floor to one side of the living
room talking. PAT thumbs through
CDs near the stereo. DIANE is in the
kitchen, building a sandwich. CAROL
ANN and KEVIN are the only two
partaking of the party. They are
dancing spiritedly with each other
and obviously enjoying themselves.
SCOTT leans against the hall
doorjamb watching them. MICKEY
and MAX are on the porch saying
good-bye to a couple of guests who
are leaving.

            MAX
    (Calling to the guests as they exit)
Thanks for coming by. Maybe we can do this again . . .
sometime soon.

          MICKEY
         (To MAX)
I hope not!
    (Starts to enter house, but stops)
This is great, Max. Really great. I don't think I've ever been
more embarrassed. And it's my birthday. Jeeze, Max. Thanks
a lot.

           (MICKEY enters the house, slamming
           the door behind her. Everyone in
           the house, except for CAROL ANN
           who continues to dance with KEVIN,
           looks at her then quickly returns to
           whatever they were doing. MICKEY

goes over and stands next SCOTT and
they both watch KEVIN and CAROL
ANN. DIANE joins them from the
kitchen eating the sandwich she has
made.)

DIANE

Great food, Mickey.

MICKEY
(Continues to watch the dancers)

Yeah, thanks.

DIANE
(Watching KEVIN and CAROL ANN)

I thought Max's sister was married.

MICKEY

She is. I thought my brother was married.

SCOTT
(As he leaves and goes to the kitchen)

He is.

(CAROL ANN and KEVIN dance over
to where MICKEY and DIANE are.)

KEVIN
(Stops dancing)

I think I need a breather. Anyone need something to drink?

CAROL ANN

I think I've got one somewhere here.
(She picks up a drink from the
bookcase.)
(KEVIN departs for the kitchen)

CAROL ANN

Isn't he cute?
(Receiving no response)
You know, Mickey, I hope you don't mind me saying so, but
this sure isn't much of a party. I've seen more fun at a . . . a .

DIANE

Tupperware party?

CAROL ANN

As a matter of fact, yes. What this party needs is more guys.

MICKEY

Oh, yeah, right.

DIANE

You know, Carol Ann, I think we have enough gay people here . . . they're just not having a gay time, if you know what I mean. We need to liven things up . . . get people going, . . . you know . . . bring people out of their corners. I mean, look at ol' Mickey here. She looks like she's just lost her best friend. Where is Max, anyway?

MICKEY

Hiding on the porch, I think.

CAROL ANN

You're right. And I know just the thing.
                 (Step toward center of the room)
Hey, everybody. We're going to play charades.

DIANE

Great idea. You ladies get things going in here and I'll get Max.

CAROL ANN
                 (Takes Diane's arm.)
Let me get her.
                 (Carol Ann goes out onto porch.)
Maxine? Aren't you going to come in and play charades with us?

MAX

I don't think so.

230

CAROL ANN

Come on . . . please? We used to have so much fun when we were kids. Remember how we used to shine the flashlight like it was a spot light and we'd take turns acting out some scene from a movie we had seen, and we would have to guess which movie ?

MAX

That was a long time ago.

CAROL ANN

Nothing is too long ago for sisters. Why don't you come on in?

MAX

Carol Ann . . . why did you come here?

CAROL ANN

Why, to see you, of course.

MAX

We haven't seen each other in two years. The only time we talk on the phone is on holidays . . . and then only sometimes. I barely remember to send you a birthday card, let alone Bobby or the boys. And then all of a sudden you show up. Why?

CAROL ANN

This sounds like an awfully serious discussion for the middle of a party.

MAX

Why did you come?

CAROL ANN

Because I didn't have any place else to go.

MAX

What do you mean you didn't have any place else to go?

CAROL ANN

Just what I said. I needed to go somewhere . . . and there just wasn't any place else to go.

(Max looks at CAROL ANN
inquisitively)
Bobby was supposed to go to another convention . . . in Dallas
this time . . . and . . . well . . . I'm pretty sure he's been seeing
someone else . . . so . . . I thought to myself, Carol Ann, if you
just up and left . . . boys and all . . . that SOB won't be able to
go anywhere. So here I am.

MAX

Carol Ann, I am sorry.

CAROL ANN

Well, I guess that's what happens when your husband's
traveling about six states and you're stuck down on the farm,
so to speak. Anyway . . . he's there and I'm here.
(Pauses)
I know my showing up without a warning kind of put a crimp
in your plans. You can't know what it means to me to be able
to come here like this. You just can't.
(Pauses)
We're sisters, Maxine. Maybe we haven't been very close
these last few years, but we're still sisters . . . and nothing can
change that . . . nothing.

MAX
(Hesitates momentarily)
Carol Ann, about what I was trying to tell you this morning
. . .

CAROL ANN

This isn't about someone dying again, is it?

MAX
(With a chuckle)
No. No one is dying.
(Haltingly)
It's a . . . it's the reason everything seems so confusing around
here . . . why Mickey and I have been snapping at each other.
. . It's just that . . . well . . .
(Finally blurts it out)
Carol Ann, I'm a lesbian.

                    CAROL ANN
                    (Matter-of-factly, without a blink of an
                    eye)
No, you're not.

                    MAX
No, really . . . I'm a lesbian . . . and Mickey is my lover.

                    CAROL ANN
Maxine, you are not a lesbian.

                    MAX
Yes I am.

                    CAROL ANN
No, you are not.

                    MAX
Yes I am, Carol Ann. I am a lesbian.

                    CAROL ANN
Maxine, if you were a lesbian, I would know it. After all, I
am your older sister and we did grow up together and I can
guarantee it . . . you-are-not-a-lesbian. Now, why don't we go
play some charades. After all, this is Mickey's birthday party,
and she is your best friend.
                    (CAROL ANN links arms with MAX
                    and guides her into the living room.
                    The women have gathered on and
                    around the couch. KEVIN and SCOTT
                    are still in the kitchen nibbling food.)

                    DIANE
All right, Max. Just in time.
                    (MAX goes over and stands by
                    MICKEY. CAROL ANN finds a place
                    on the couch.)

                    MAX
                    (Quietly to MICKEY)
I told her.

MICKEY
(A little too loud)

You did!

(Quieter)

You did.

MAX

Uh- huh.

MICKEY

And . . . ?

MAX

She doesn't believe me.

MICKEY

She doesn't believe you?

MAX

She told me that if I were a lesbian, she'd know it . . . and she
doesn't . . . so I'm not. So whose turn is it?

About the Author

olivia free-woman has been writing since she fell in love with her first spiral-bound journal in high school. Her work includes plays, poetry, articles, and short stories for children and adults. Her first play, *An Interruption*, was selected as the first place winner in a competition sponsored by Arizona State University Women and the American Association of University Women and produced in Tempe. She has been published by the ASU College of Education, in the women's news journal *off our backs*, and in several local publications including *WICCE* and *Dimensions*. An educator for thirty-one years, olivia was an "out" teacher at a central city school in Phoenix. She taught eighth grade math, science and whatever else.

She was active in the women's community since shortly after her return to Phoenix from Missouri in 1978. As a member of Phoenix Women Take Back the Night, the Phoenix Women's Center, AZ Women for Reproductive Rights, Aunt Pearl and the Lesbian Resource Project, she was instrumental in organizing political rallies, marches, demonstrations and cultural events. She was also a peace keeper for a number of events locally and in Tucson including the first Lesbian and Gay Rights marches in the Valley. A poet and author with twenty years of voice lessons behind her, she was pleased to have the opportunity to share her writing through *Fine China and Molotov Cocktails*, a writers group she participated in for eight years, and to sing with *TLC*.

olivia died on 2 April 2010 after a short illness at a much too young age. She was born, raised, and lived in Sunnyslope, part of Phoenix, Arizona, and was formerly known as Judy Canion.

Proceeds from the sale of this book will go to the olivia free-woman Educational Scholarship fund to assist students from Creighton Elementary School in Phoenix, Arizona in pursuit of higher education.